Implementing
Client/Server
Computing

Other Books by McGraw-Hill

Implementing Client/Server Computing

A Strategic Perspective

Bernard H. Boar

McGraw-Hill, Inc.

New York   St. Louis   San Francisco   Auckland   Bogotá
Caracas   Lisbon   London   Madrid   Mexico   Milan
Montreal   New Delhi   Paris   San Juan   São Paulo
Singapore   Sydney   Tokyo   Toronto

Library of Congress Cataloging-in-Publication Data

Boar, Bernard H.
    Implementing client/server computing : a strategic perspective /
Bernard H. Boar.
        p.   cm.
    Includes index.
    ISBN 0-07-006215-3
    1. System design. 2. Application software. I. Title.
QA76.9.S88564 1992
658.4'038'0285436—dc20   82-26688
                                                              CIP

1 2 3 4 5 6 7 8 9 0   DOC/DOC   9 8 7 6 5 4 3 2

ISBN 0-07-006215-3

*The sponsoring editor for this book was Jeanne Glasser and the
production supervisor was Donald F. Schmidt. This book was set in
Century Schoolbook by North Market Street Graphics. Printed and
bound by R. R. Donnelley & Sons Company.*

*To Diane, Jessica, and Debbie
with love always*

Contents

Foreword

In the Information Management Services Division of the American Telephone & Telegraph Company, we use our information technology expertise for one purpose: "to help AT&T win in the marketplace." AT&T's business units are engaged in global competition, and winning in that global marketplace requires the timely and efficient use of *information movement* and *management* technologies. There are fewer and fewer applications where the source of differentiation to the customer or advantage over a competitor is not partially or fully rooted in the purposeful application of information technology. Just as we suggest for our external clients, we infuse information technology into our own business practices to offer products and services that make us consistently superior to our competitors.

Advantage is, unfortunately, only transitory. Nowhere is this more true than in the information movement and management area. The pace of change quickens continually, and future business advantages will go to those organizations that more quickly and purposefully integrate new technologies into the technology portfolio to allow improved linkage between business needs and information technology solutions.

As business managers responsible for the constant infusion of new, advantageous technologies for use by our internal AT&T business units, we have come to appreciate the difference between incremental change and discontinuous change. Incremental change can be handled with normal technology transfer procedures; discontinuous change, a paradigm shift, requires much more effort. A paradigm shift requires a rethinking and a reengineering of the organization. Paradigm shifts are difficult times to manage due to the disruption they cause but, for the same reason, are exciting times because of the opportunities they provide.

This book is about the paradigm shift from host-centered computing, which has dominated commercial data processing for the past 25 years, to client/server computing, which will dominate commercial data processing for at least the next decade. We have been intimately involved in managing that paradigm shift at AT&T and, having experienced firsthand the challenges, frustrations, and excitement, are pleased to be associated with a work that can expedite the change for others. This book is unique in how it blends the disciplines of strategic thinking and information management. Information managers need to understand both the technology issues and the strategic business advantages that client/server computing offers.

We are well on our way to implementing client/server computing at AT&T. We are excited about the future and believe that a radical reengineering of the business will now be possible in ways unforeseen only a few years ago. While transforming such a large organization from the host-centered computing paradigm to the client/server model is a momentous task, we are enthusiastic about the journey and hope that you join the transition.

B. P. Donohue, III

Bart P. Donohue III
Vice President,
Product Management & Engineering
Information Management Services
AT&T

Samuel V. Coursen

Sam S. Coursen
Division Manager,
Processing Product Line
Information Management Services
AT&T

Ben Doyle

Ben Doyle
Division Manager,
Product Engineering
Information Management Services
AT&T

Preface

As one's career progresses, the problems and challenges that are presented grow considerably in dimension. When I wrote my first book, *Abend Debugging for COBOL Programmers,* in the 1970s, the problem and challenge were pretty straightforward: how do you read an OS/MVT core dump? The problem was terribly practical and immediate. As was true with many of my colleagues of the era, my programming skills were less than perfect and an ABEND was not that unusual an event. The complexity of debugging it, however, was incredible, given the myriad of hieroglyphic control blocks and endless pages of dumped memory locations presented. The problem was, however, quite solvable and, with much practice (unfortunately my programs dumped often), I rose to the challenge and became quite proficient in "dump" reading, which culminated in my first book.

Time and opportunity marched on, my debugging skills atrophied, and, in the 1980s, I found myself confronted with quite a different problem. The problem and challenge now were requirements definition. How do you develop a correct set of specifications for a business application? My answer to this was presented in my second book, *Application Prototyping: A Requirements Definition Strategy for the 80s.* The basic thesis of this book was that the essential problem of requirements definition was one of communication—i.e., none of the participants in the development process really understood each other, and the then advocated communication media (structure charts, data flow diagrams, structured English, etc.) was simply too passive to stimulate and animate the requirements-gathering exchange. The proposal, software prototyping, was really quite simple: build a model of the application—quickly and in context. This is essentially what the engineering professions had done for centuries. Invest neither substantial time nor money in developing a finished application until a working prototype has been experienced by and agreed to by the user. While at the time this was an incredibly controversial proposal (it was the height of the "structured" era and if it wasn't structured, it was heresy), I am glad to observe that it is now quite a respected and accepted part of the systems development process. Fred Brooks was right: ". . . plan to throw one away, you will anyhow."* The problem and challenge was bigger but, again, quite solvable.

As I find myself in the 1990s, the problems and challenges continue to grow greater in scope and importance to the business. This time the question is one of architecture. How should one arrange the topology of the information-processing technology assets of the corporation to maximize their contribution to the company's competitive advantage? Given the diverse needs of the user community, the incredible and constantly growing continuum of information technology, and the demands of senior management for a visible return on their information investment, how do you position yourself architecturally for maximum advantage? What makes an information architecture advantageous? What is your information architecture strategy to be?

---

* *The Mythical Man Month,* Fred Brooks, Addison Wesley, 1975.

This book is my response to this problem. I believe the answer to this challenge is the *client/server computing architecture*. Client/server computing is a processing model in which a single application is partitioned between multiple processors (front-end and back-end), and the processors cooperate (transparent to the end user) to complete the processing as a single unified task. A client/server bond product ties the processors together to provide a single system image (illusion). Shareable resources are positioned as servers offering one or more services. Applications (requestors) are positioned as clients which access authorized services. The entire architecture is endlessly recursive; in turn, servers can become clients and request services of other servers on the network and so on. The client/server computing architecture offers the maximum advantage to those responsible for making the corporate-systems architecture decision. The problem and challenge are the greatest yet, but again, quite solvable.

I recall, as an undergraduate in the Engineering School of City College of New York, taking a course entitled "Thermodynamics I." A concept impressed on us in this course was the inevitable tendency of systems, left unchecked, to move toward disorder. Left on their own, without vigilance and control, systems will naturally migrate to a complete state of chaos. The term used to describe this phenomenon is *entropy*.

As an information technology strategist for my employer, I had often felt that my world was involved in a world-class march toward entropy, until I appreciated the opportunity of client/server computing. How could one make sense and bring order out of the plethora of information-technology products available (and growing at an apparently exponential rate) that seemed contradictory, redundant, noninteroperable, and impossible to integrate? With users requiring ever more specific information appliances to enable their specific business practices, how could or would we ever weave all the technology together into a coherent and purposeful whole? Information technology, as we started the 1990s, clearly looked like the Harvard Business School case study on entropy.

If you have any reason to doubt this assessment, I suggest that you simply store your collection of industry magazines, vendor announcements, and industry show literature for a few weeks. As you, in one session, browse through the stack, notice the total lack of coherency or context. How does one make sense and bring order out of it all? How do we act to preempt entropy? Obviously, I suggest that the action we take is to build our information architecture on the client/server computing model. Client/server computing offers the only option to bring order to the paradox of the dispersion of processing and, simultaneously, the ever-greater need for sharing and interoperability.

This book looks at client/server computing from a business management perspective. It deals with technical issues only from the conceptual framework viewpoint. The reason for this is twofold. First, it is my view that the information architecture of a business is a strategic business decision, not a technical decision, and, as such, should be analyzed and selected from the management context. Secondly, there exists an endless amount of detailed technical information on client/server products but a paucity of analysis on what critical business needs they really solve. There is a desperate need for the merging of technology opportunity with proper strategic analysis. We will, consequently, look at client/server computing from the perspectives of strategic intent, core competencies, competitive advantage, and critical business practices rather than the perspective of network protocols, relational database management systems, UNIX operating systems, symmetric multiprocessors, or microprocessors. What is important about client/server computing is not what it can do in a technological sense, but what it can do for the business.

In 1990, the information management and movement industry will be a \$530 billion worldwide business. For what purpose are users expending such enormous funds? What is the enduring need that drives businesses year after year to invest and reinvest in information technology? I submit that the goal that business seeks to meet with information technology is total systems maneuverability: the ability to act preemptively or react defensively to the vicissitudes of the competitive marketplace. Business demands the ability to "play the game" on an enabling information infrastructure that allows the maximum sharing of all forms of information to increasingly dispersed and mobile users. The information technology capability may never block a business initiative and, to the contrary, should provide a wealth of information-system alternative implementations for the business strategist to choose from. This is why business invests and reinvests staggering sums of money in information movement and management technology, and it is to achieve that end that client/server computing is of strategic importance. It provides the underlying information-processing architecture to permit the information asset to achieve this desired and required level of system maneuverability.

This book should be of interest to managers responsible for strategic information systems planning, systems architecture, product planning, application design, system analyst, and/or chief information officer support. It will not be of interest to individuals primarily interested in technical details.

That same semester that I learned of the notion of entropy, I also took a course in the "Mathematics of Computer Science." What we did in this course was to do proofs of theorems. A theorem would be postulated, and we had to do one of the following:

1. Prove it was true by logical deduction.
2. Prove it was true by logical induction.
3. Prove it was false by counterexample, i.e., demonstrate a case where the premise of the theorem was true, but not the conclusion.

This book will attempt to prove the following theorem:

> If you wish to position your enterprise for maximum competitive advantage through information technology, then you need to strategically implement the client/server computing architecture.

Acceptance of the theorem or the derivation of the counterexample is your assignment.

Bernard H. Boar

Acknowledgments

At the Information Management Services Division of AT&T, our planning and operational execution is performed within a management system called Total Quality Management (TQM). TQM is devoted to continuous improvement in the quality of the products and services we deliver to our customers, the AT&T business units and divisions. An integral component of TQM is empowerment to teams.

Some material presented in this book originated as part of work that was done by various strategy teams. Though the material presented here is considerably amplified and matured in its completeness, I would like to recognize the contribution of the individuals on the following teams to my understanding of the subject area:

- Database Strategy Team
- Information Processing Strategy Team
- Data Processing Organization Design Team
- Processing Product Line Strategy Team

All the people who worked on these efforts influenced my thinking.

There are, however, three executives who require explicit citation. Bart Donohue, Sam Coursen, and Ben Doyle have demonstrated exemplary information-technology leadership in positioning our organization for the future. Their influence, energy, and ideas have clarified many issues for me and set the direction for our organization for years to come. I thank them for their help and assistance.

I would like to acknowledge the work of the many original thinkers upon whose foundation ideas this book builds. This book is not so much creation as it is integration. The original contributions are cited appropriately throughout the book. My value added, hopefully, is holistic thinking that has combined these discrete ideas into a purposeful whole.

Lastly I would like to recommend that the reader take the time to read both *The Art of War* by Sun Tzu and *The Prince* by Machiavelli. Both are books that, though brief, provide incredible insight into strategy formulation that will prove invaluable in understanding how and when to apply information technology to the business. Throughout this book, both authors are quoted.

Bernard H. Boar

Implementing
Client/Server
Computing

Introduction

1.1 Purpose

The purpose of this book is to provide a management assessment of the competitive business advantages that can be accrued by constructing the corporation's information systems architecture on a client/server computing infrastructure. It is the thesis of this book that Client/Server Computing (CSC) represents a new, different, and advantageous capability that permits both novel and better (cheaper, faster, and/or improved feature/function) solutions to be applied to the business practices of the enterprise. Client/server computing enables Information Movement and Management (IM&M—aka information technology) assets (voice, data connectivity, processing, and data) to be unified and connected for the first time. If reacted to with an appropriate strategic response, this has tremendous implications in terms of improving the company's competitive position.

IM&M, or *Information Technology (I/T),* is the asset/capability base on which the enterprise constructs its business information systems. IM&M may be more rigorously defined as follows:

> *Information Movement and Management* is the preparation, collection, transport, retrieval, storage, access, presentation, and transformation of information in all its forms (voice, graphics, text, video, and image). Movement can take place between humans, humans and machines, and/or between machines. Management assures the proper selection, deployment, administration, operation, maintenance, and evolution of the IM&M assets consistent with organizational goals and objectives.

Figure 1.1 illustrates this definition. IM&M encompasses the following variables:

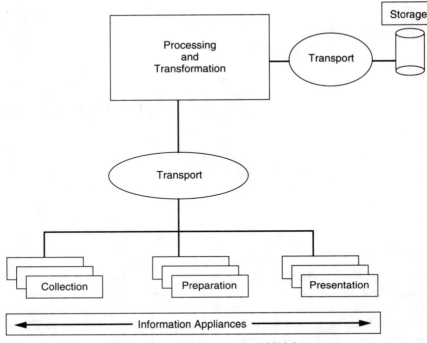

Figure 1.1   Information Movement and Management Model.

- the variety of information collection, preparation, and presentation appliances
- the geographical distribution/demographics of the senders/receivers of information
- the availability of the IM&M asset for use
- the standards used to enable the productive use of the IM&M asset
- the translation of information between IM&M components
- the asset scalability (i.e., performance, cost, volume, total users, and total concurrent users)
- the transparency of change
- the accessibility of the IM&M asset
- component to component integration

Implicitly (without forethought) or explicitly (by planned intention), IM&M applications are constructed within the framework of a systems architecture that defines the overall structure and relationships of the application portfolio. The inherent "power" of the chosen architecture defines, in whole or in part, the attributes of the applications, i.e., maintainability, flexibility, modularity, scalability, adaptability, portability, and interoperability.

The architecture is often the primary determinant of the application's ability to "change." A rigid architecture pre-positions the enterprise to expensive, time-consuming, and painful change. A flexible architecture positions the enterprise for continuous system evolution. The enterprise can either be positioned for failure through rigidity or winning through continuous reaction and adaptability to the dynamics of customers, suppliers, and competitors. Competitive position can be markedly enriched or impoverished by the architecture decision.

Historically, the prevailing architecture used for building business applications has been the host-centered computing architecture (see Fig. 1.2). In this arrangement, a user would enter transactions at a dumb-terminal (i.e., the terminal has no processing capability). At the completion of entry, the transaction would be processed by the host (presentation logic, algorithmic/business rule logic, and data manipulation [add, modify, retrieve, and delete]) and the results returned to the user to complete the transaction cycle. It is well worth noting that while the processing "revolutions" of the last fifteen years (the addi-

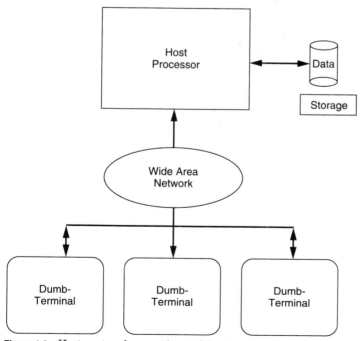

Figure 1.2   Host-centered computing architecture.

tions of minicomputers and personal computers to the original main-frame-only environment) have altered the sizing, price/performance, software feature/functionality, and geographic relationship of the user to the computing resource, they did not materially alter this architecture model; they simply scaled it down (albeit to considerable advantage). Figure 1.3 illustrates this observation.

Figure 1.4 illustrates the client/server computing model. *Client/server computing* may be defined as follows:

> *Client/server computing* is a processing model in which a single application is partitioned between multiple processors (front-end and back-end) and the processors cooperate (transparent to the end user) to complete the processing as a single unified task. A client/server bond product ties the processors together to provide a single system image (illusion). Shareable resources are positioned as servers offering one or more services. Applications are positioned as requestor clients that access authorized services. The architecture is endlessly recursive; in turn, servers can become clients and request services of other servers on the network and so on and so on.

Client/server computing creates a network of processors that work together interactively, as one, to complete business transactions. If we use the term *information appliance* to denote a computing capability embedded in an information presentation, collection, and/or preparation device, it becomes clear that client/server computing permits computing intelligence to be distributed throughout the enterprise at selected scale and functionality levels and, concurrently, for the first time, to be unified and interconnected.

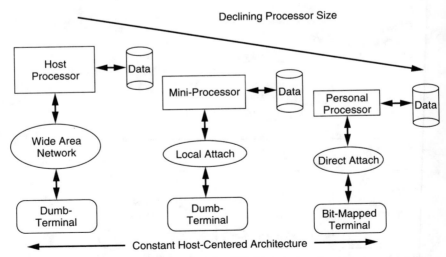

Figure 1.3   Staying power of host-centered architecture.

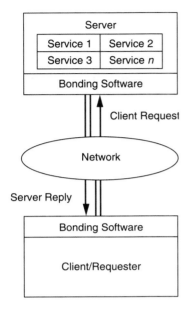

Figure 1.4   Client/server computing architecture.

It will be the purpose of this book to examine the rationale for and implications of migrating the corporate information systems architecture to client/server computing from host-centered computing. Figure 1.5 illustrates this inevitability. The perspective taken in developing our arguments will be that of strategic manager, not technologist. Client/server computing, as will be demonstrated, offers such opportunity for competitive advantage that it needs to be managed and implemented as a strategic business initiative—not simply another new technology introduction. The IM&M delivery capability of the corporation is increasingly becoming the critical enabler to superior customer service, world-class market research, timely product development, and best-of-breed operations management. Advantage equates to IM&M advantage. Client/server computing can enable the enterprise to position itself for immediate competitive advantage and to be adaptable for future advantage. It can enable the enterprise to compound advantage by rapidly adding advantage on top of advantage, providing a hopelessly moving target for competitors. Such roots of competitive advantage need to be orchestrated from the strategic viewpoint.

1.2   Analytical Models

This book relies heavily on the use of analytical models to present and integrate its ideas. Analytical models provide a framework for repre-

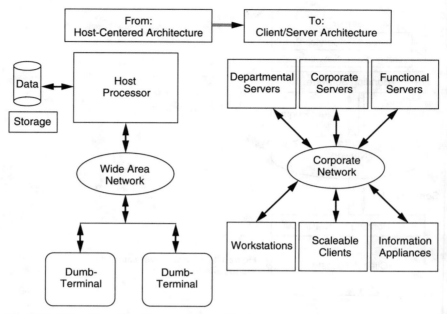

Figure 1.5   Migration of business system architecture.

senting and understanding the entire problem, as well as the individual parts and their relationships. They enable improved comprehension since we can first agree on the validity of the abstraction (the model) and then carry that agreement forward to the immediate problem. Models bring order, clarity, and structure to the debate.

Strategic analysis requires holistic thinking: combining what has not necessarily been related before. Consequently, this book employs and integrates many discrete models to construct its arguments. It is a tribute to the insight of the original creators of the models that the definitions were so refined that they could easily be synthesized together for an unforeseen purpose.

The following models are used in this book:

- *Five Forces Model:*   Used to analyze the competitive health of an enterprise.

- *Processing Architecture Models:*   Used to illustrate the structure of IM&M system architectures.

- *Data Architecture Models:*   Used to illustrate the structure of the data stores used to manage the enterprise's data asset.

- *Strategic Analysis Model:*   Used to illustrate the process of developing strategic objectives and enabling strategies for the enterprise.

- *Data Model:*   Used to illustrate business entities and their interrelationships.

- *7 "S" Model:*   Used to decide what implementation programs are required to implement a strategy.

- *Engineering Model:*   Used to illustrate how technology evolves from an initial craft state to an engineering discipline.

- *Core Competency Model:*   Used to analyze what core competencies/capabilities an organization must have to execute a strategy.

- *Medical Model:*   Used to diagnose the illnesses preventing the effective use of IM&M by the enterprise.

- *Configuration Model:*   Used to illustrate the complexity of managing client/server solutions.

The models will be explained when they are introduced. I suggest you spend time thinking about the models, including reading the cited references, since deeper understanding of the models enables more insightful understanding of the architecture question.

I have always found models fascinating, and my prior book on prototyping advocated the construction of application models as a superior strategy for requirements analysis. Software prototypes are animated models that are fun to play with. The models used in this book are not animated; they are thinking models to enable clarity of thought and expression. They are not as much fun; comprehension is hard work. But then again, the problem is different, being one of insight and not of demonstration.

1.3 Book Overview

The remainder of this book will build on the initial ideas introduced in this chapter and fully explain the competitive advantages offered by client/server computing. This will be accomplished in the following manner:

- *Chapter 2: "The Management Perspective."*   This chapter will explain what is meant by a management perspective. IM&M can be viewed in innumerable ways: from the perspective of the database administrator, communications planner, operations manager, end user, data administrator, etc. The management perspective defines the context from which issues are viewed and analyzed.

- *Chapter 3: "Business Competition."*   This chapter will introduce and explain the Five Forces Model as a method to analyze the competitive situation of an enterprise. It also will suggest that business con-

ditions in the 1990s will exaggerate the importance of certain implications of the model. The Five Forces Model will be used extensively
in Chap. 6, "The Business Problem," to measure the true impact
of IM&M problems on the competitive well being of the enterprise,
and Chap. 7, "Client/Server Computing," to demonstrate how
client/server computing alleviates those problems. We define corporate health as equating to competitive health.

- *Chapter 4: "IM&M Architecture."* This chapter will develop an
  understanding of what is meant by an IM&M architecture and how
  to distinguish between multiple candidates for utility. Since
  client/server computing is an architecture, this chapter provides the
  necessary foundation knowledge to appreciate the characteristics
  and role of an architecture.

- *Chapter 5: "Critical Issues of Information Systems."* This chapter
  will analyze the critical issues that information system executives
  have identified as crucial to their enterprise's well being. The degree
  to which an architecture enables or blocks the achievement of these
  objectives is another measure of the utility of the architecture.

- *Chapter 6: "The Business Problem."* This chapter will explain the
  current IM&M illnesses that are preventing the effective use of
  IM&M for advantage. The Medical Model will be used to decompose
  each illness into symptoms, pathology, and etiology. To decide the
  degree of illness, two methods will be used:

  1. The Five Forces Model (see Chap. 2) will be used to analyze how
     the IM&M problems debilitate corporate competitive health.

  2. The critical issues (see Chap. 5) will be used to learn to what
     degree the IM&M problems block the achievement of the critical
     IM&M objectives.

  At the completion of this chapter, the reader will have a thorough
  appreciation of the competitive disadvantages that the current
  IM&M problems impose on the enterprise.

- *Chapter 7: "Client/Server Computing."* This chapter will describe
  client/server computing. An exhaustive analysis will be made that
  will demonstrate the business benefits of client/server computing
  and how it provides therapeutic treatment for the problems diagnosed in Chap. 6.

- *Chapter 8: "Implementing Client/Server Computing."* This chapter
  will analyze the issues surrounding the strategic implementation of
  client/server computing within the enterprise. The 7 "S" Model will
  be used as the framework for identifying areas requiring implementation attention. At the completion of this chapter, the reader will

have a thorough understanding of what actions are required to implement client/server computing strategically.

- *Chapter 9: "Epilogue."* Final thoughts on strategy and client/server computing.

The overall structure of the book is illustrated in Fig. 1.6 and may be understood as follows:

- *Foundation.* Chapters 2–5 build a foundation of common knowledge. It assures that we all share the same view of competitive analysis, the management perspective, IM&M architecture, and critical information system issues. It establishes a "level playing field" for all readers.

- *Problem.* Chapter 6 analyzes the problems inhibiting the effective deployment of IM&M and the consequences to the health of the enterprise.

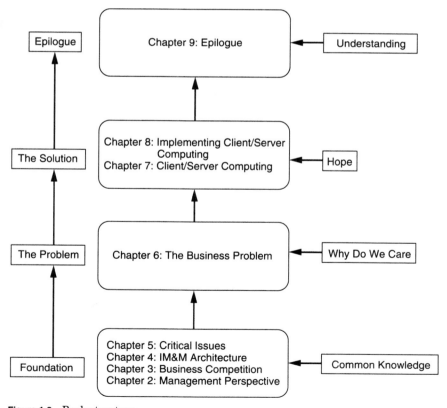

Figure 1.6 Book structure.

- *Solution.*   Chapters 7 and 8 explain the solution that client/server computing offers and the issues surrounding its effective implementation.

- *Epilogue.*   Chapter 9 provides final thoughts on IM&M, client/server computing, and strategy.

There is little doubt as to the ascendancy of client/server computing as the preferred processing architecture within this decade. The issue becomes whether you plan and manage an attractive implementation or it happens to you; whether the architectural mistakes of the 1970s and 1980s are repeated or an elegant solution is implemented.

2

The Management Perspective

The purpose of this chapter is to explain the management perspective (as opposed to a technologist perspective) and why strategic management of client/server computing is so important. Why not treat client/server computing as just another technology and leave its introduction to normal technology transfer procedures? Why not simply treat it the same way that the addition of a new screen generator, spreadsheet, editor, or report writer is treated? Why is it so special that it requires strategic management? To answer these questions, we will do the following:

- *Section 2.1: Strategic Management.* We will develop a model of strategic management.

- *Section 2.2: The Management Perspective.* We will develop a model that links IM&M to the business (a management perspective).

- *Section 2.3: The Technologist Perspective.* We will develop a model that links the business to IM&M (a technologist perspective).

- *Section 2.4: Synthesis.* We will compare the two models and understand why client/server will require a strategic implementation.

At the completion of this chapter, the reader should have a thorough understanding of the importance of linking IM&M technology to the business instead of linking the business to IM&M technology.

2.1 Strategic Management

Strategic management refers to the discipline by which strategic objectives and strategies are developed to guide the long-term direction of the enterprise. *Strategic* implies that the item is of major consequence, that its accomplishment is imperative and will have a lasting impact. If it is strategic, it is critical to the long-term well being of the company and will often require many changes throughout the organization. Strategic issues are managed by the executive council of the enterprise. The strategic planning exercise provides a means to infuse strategic thinking as daily thinking throughout the management team.

Figure 2.1 provides an initial view of the strategic planning process. (It will be extended later in the book.) It can be understood as follows:

1. Data is collected by strategic area for both *internal* (about the company) and *external* (the environment that impacts the company) analysis. Representative strategic areas are competition, markets, human resources, products, management systems, and methods of sales. Analytical methods such as opportunity/threat analysis, strength/weakness analysis, critical success factors, and Five Forces analysis are used to interpret the data and develop insight into both the current and evolving situation. This entire process of

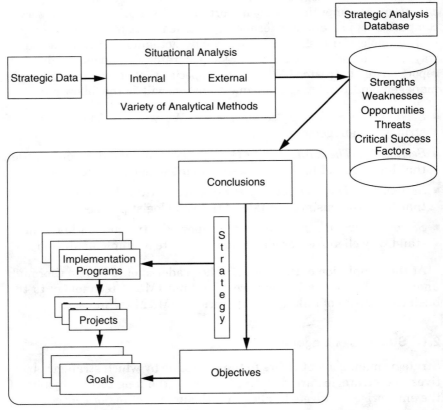

Figure 2.1   Strategic Planning Model I.

data collection and analysis is called *situational analysis* and results in the creation of a database to serve as a fact repository for making decisions. There is agreement upon where the enterprise is, its situation, and the anticipated changes with which it must deal during the planning period.

Table 2.1 identifies a starting set of subjects that are reviewed during situational analysis. The set of results from the analysis of each area is joined to create the notion of a "position." The enterprise can be viewed as at time T being in position P where P is the set of individual positions for each strategic area, i.e., $P_{\text{enterprise}} = (P_{\text{markets}}, P_{\text{product}}, P_{\text{finance}}, P_{\text{etc.}})$. The concept of position is completely recursive; a given position is composed of n subpositions. The notion of position will be used in Chap. 8, "Implementing Client/Server Computing," to understand the implementation issues surrounding moving the enterprise from $P_{\text{prior client/server computing}}$ to $P_{\text{client/server computing}}$. Positions are best expressed graphically, quantitatively, and, lastly, qualitatively. While P_{finance} (financial position) is the most common way of expressing position (i.e., $P_{\text{finance}} = (P_{\text{earnings per share}}, P_{\text{margins}}, P_{\text{profitability}}, P_{\text{expense/employee}}, P_{\text{revenue/employee}}$, etc.), the other strategic areas also can be positioned. Figure 2.2 illustrates three ways that the position of the organization's products and services may be illustrated.

2. Conclusions are reached on items requiring a strategic response or initiative. What are the primary issues requiring attention in this planning period?

TABLE 2.1   Strategic Areas

Strategic Planning Concerns Itself with the Major Strategic Areas of the Business

Strategic area	Internal analysis	External analysis
Products/services	X	
Markets	X	X
Customers	X	X
Technology	X	
Production methods	X	
Method of sale	X	
Method of distribution	X	
Natural resources	X	X
Suppliers		X
Human resources	X	
Organization structure	X	
Management systems	X	
External environment (socioeconomic factors)		X
Information systems	X	
Finances	X	
Competition		X
Industry		X

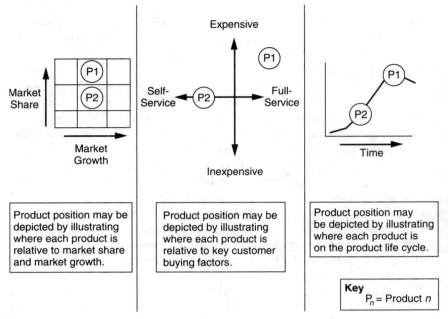

Figure 2.2   Product position.

3. Objectives are defined. They identify where the enterprise needs to be: What is to be accomplished by the end of this planning period? They are specific, measurable, and dated. They will culminate in the obtainment of a new position.

4. Strategies are developed that are purposeful and coherent actions to achieve the objectives. Strategies are the means by which we move from where we are, the *conclusions,* to where we want to be, the *objectives.* Strategies are purposeful in that they independently represent specific actions to achieve an objective. They are coherent in that they support each other and provide synergy in achieving the objectives. Strategies may be differentiated from conclusions in that conclusions are descriptive while strategies are prescriptive.

5. Strategies are made operational through implementation programs that are targeted to execute projects. Implementation programs achieve interim goals that are milestones on the way to reaching the objectives. The implementation programs move us from our current position to the desired one. Implementation programs are composed of multiple projects.

Strategic planning permits one to understand and assess the situation.

So it is said that if you know others and know yourself, you will not be imperiled in a hundred battles; if you do not know others but know yourself, you win one and lose one; if you do not know others and do not know yourself, you will be imperiled in every single battle. . . . Having established these comparisons, you will have a preview of superiorities and inferiorities, weaknesses and strengths; this will enable you to prevail.*

Of particular importance throughout the strategic planning process is the assessment and planning for the organization's *sustainable competitive advantage (SCA)*. The SCA is the resource, capability, asset, process, etc. that provides an enterprise with a distinct attraction to its customers and unique advantage over its competitors. While an SCA does not guarantee market success, it is a prerequisite for success. An ideal SCA can be identified by seven attributes:

- *Customer perception.*   The customer perceives a consistent difference in an important buying factor for the product.

- *Linkage.*   The difference in customer perception is directly related to the SCA.

- *Durability.*   The differential customer perception and SCA linkage is durable over an extended period of time.

- *Transparency.*   The mechanics/details of the SCA are difficult for a competitor to understand.

- *Accessibility.*   A competitor, even if the SCA is transparent, has unequal access to the resources required to duplicate the SCA.

- *Replication.*   A competitor, even if the SCA is transparent, would have extreme difficulty in replicating the SCA.

- *Coordination.*   The SCA requires difficult and subtle coordination of extensive resources.

Table 2.2 can be used to evaluate a candidate SCA for utility. We will use this matrix in Chap. 7 to evaluate how the IM&M organization infuses its implementation of client/server computing with competitive advantage for the firm.

When it is asserted that client/server computing requires "strategic management," what is being suggested is that client/server computing is a strategy that needs to be understood, managed, and implemented within the context of Fig. 2.1. This approach will be further amplified in Chap. 8, "Implementing Client/Server Computing."

---

* *The Art of War,* Sun-Tzu, translated by Thomas Cleary, Shambhala Dragon Editions, 1988.

TABLE 2.2   SCA Evaluation Matrix

Candidate Sustainable Competitive Advantages Can Be Evaluated by Using This Matrix

SCA attribute	Candidate SCA		
	SCA 1	SCA 2	SCA 3
Customer perception			
SCA linkage			
Durability			
Transparency			
Accessibility			
Replication			
Coordination			

2.2   Management Perspective

Figure 2.3 illustrates the structure of the enterprise and the linkage (relationship) of IM&M to that structure. Figure 2.3 can be understood as follows:

1. A business has a business scope that defines the major attributes and boundaries of the business. A typical business scope is illustrated in Table 2.3. The business scope summarizes the key describers of the business.

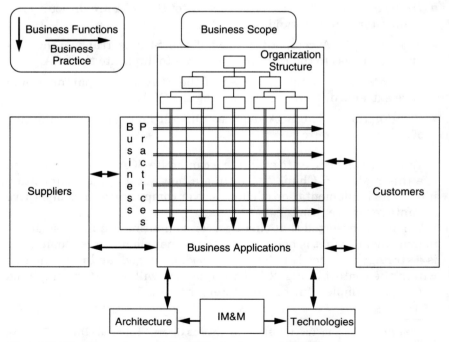

Figure 2.3   Management perspective of the business and IM&M.

TABLE 2.3   Model Business Scope

The Business Scope Defines the Key Attributes of the Business

Business scope attribute	Attribute definition
Mission	The purpose of the business
Values	What the business believes in
Customers/markets	To whom do we sell?
Geography	Where do we sell?
Products/services	What do we sell?
Strategic intent	What is the long term ambition of our actions?
Driving force	What is the primary determiner of the products and services we sell?
Sustainable competitive advantage	What about us attracts us to customers and deters competitors?

2. The business organizes itself into functional units to realize its mission. (In Chap. 8, "Implementing Client/Server Computing," we will discuss how information systems should organize to support client/server computing.)

3. An organization unit performs one or more functions. The business delivers products/services and operates itself by executing business practices that are horizontal collections of functions. The practices work toward achieving internal organization objectives as well as interfacing with external entities (customers and suppliers). Some business practices are exceedingly important to the enterprise and are denoted as *critical business practices*. A critical business practice is a process that the enterprise must perform in a superior manner if it is to compete successfully. Business practices are decomposable into capabilities that represent enduring requirements for the practice.

4. The business practice capabilities are automated as business applications which use appropriate IM&M to accrue advantage in their execution. The benefit may be one of economics, timeliness, capability, volume, service level, reliability, responsiveness, etc. While the capability requirements of a business practice may remain constant over an extended period, the method of solution is dynamic with available technology and is the source of changing advantage. It's as though one can give the same final examination each year without concern for cheating since, although the questions remain the same, the answers change. The applications are developed on an IM&M architecture using available technology to optimize the application.

Figure 2.4 illustrates more deeply the management perspective. It should be read as follows:

1. A business practice requires many capabilities to execute.

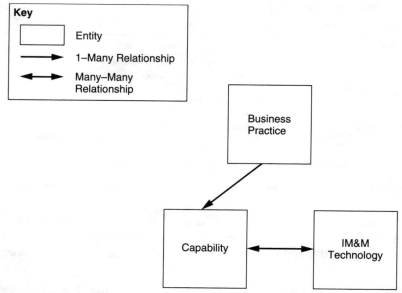

Figure 2.4   Magnified business practice IM&M relationship.

2. Each capability is automated through a chosen set of advantageous IM&M technologies.

3. IM&M technologies may be used advantageously by multiple capabilities of one or more business practices.

Table 2.4 shows this point. Remember that all practices are not equal and technologies that support critical business practices are by association more important to the enterprise than technologies that do not. Also, again notice that capability fulfillment normally requires the integration of more than one technology, and a given technology will be used to enable multiple capabilities. A technology that can be reused to enable multiple practices, particularly critical practices, is a high leverage technology.

The management perspective of the relationship/linkage between the business and IM&M is, therefore, as follows:

1. The objective of the business is to realize its mission.

2. The business organizes to do so.

3. Business practices are the vehicle by which functional units join together to deliver a product/service.

4. Business practices are automated as business applications to maximize advantage by selecting appropriate IM&M solutions.

5. *The purpose of IM&M is to enable the business practices.*

TABLE 2.4   Relating Technologies to Business Practices

IM&M Technologies Provide Solutions to Enable Business Practice Capabilities to Be Executed in a Superior Manner

Business practice	Capability	IM&M technology
Providing low-cost customized products	Rapidly configure customized complex solutions	1. Expert systems 2. Object-oriented databases 3. Computer-based training
	Rapidly design and implement software customizations	1. Expert systems 2. Object-oriented programming
	Efficient installation and assembly	1. Portable computers 2. Computer-based training 3. Expert systems
Shorten product development cycle time	Link product development personnel and processes	1. Electronic mail 2. Image processing 3. Groupware 4. Video-conferencing
	Support development process	1. Expert systems 2. Groupware 3. Multimedia systems
Superior market segmentation	Detailed customer analysis	1. Expert systems 2. Relational databases 3. Very large databases 4. Sophisticated graphical user interfaces 5. Electronic mail 6. Multimedia

IM&M solutions must be linked to a business practice for the purpose of achieving advantage. The business practice comes first.

2.3   Technologist Perspective

Figure 2.5 illustrates the relationship/linkage of the business to IM&M from the view of a technologist. Figure 2.5 can be interpreted as follows:

1. IM&M as a technical discipline offers both architectures and specific technologies.
2. The technologies have features/functions/capabilities that can enable the movement and management of information.
3. The technologist decides which technologies are "ready" to be used.
4. The business should use the technologies to build applications.

IM&M, as though it exists for its own sake, comes first. This perspective understands technology but does not understand the need or

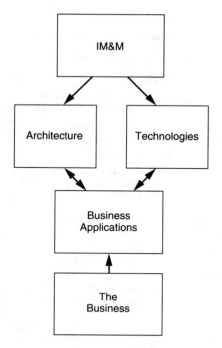

Figure 2.5 Technologist perpec-
tive of IM&M and the business.

priority that it be linked to the automation of business practices. While the technologist understands that the technologies will be used to build applications, he or she does not appreciate the roots from which the applications grow.

2.4 Synthesis

The difference between the two perspectives is pronounced. The management perspective views IM&M as another corporate resource to be used to achieve the corporate mission and strategic intent. The technologist perspective is fascinated with technology for technology's sake. Though this is fun for the technologist, it makes the direct linking of technology to business requirements a random activity rather than a directed one.

Now that we understand why it is important to view IM&M from a management perspective, why is it so important to manage client/server computing strategically? In Chap. 6, "The Business Problem," evidence will be presented to show that the application portfolio is in serious trouble; there exist deeply rooted and enormous problems with the effective use of IM&M to meet business needs. A large percentage of these problems can be traced to the multitude of IM&M

architectures that are used and their "weakness." If a "powerful" architecture existed (flexible, modular, expandable, scalable, etc.), then Fig. 2.3 could be recast as illustrated in Figure 2.6. In this portrayal, the architecture is the foundation and building block of the entire application portfolio. It pre-positions the applications for advantage since the applications inherit the advantages of the powerful architecture on which they are built. This is the critical point. Since IM&M is so important to the competitive health of the enterprise, the identification and implementation of a powerful architecture that pre-positions the application portfolio for winning is of strategic merit.

We conclude from the arguments made in this chapter the following:

1. Strategic management provides the context for overseeing activities of critical importance to the long-term health of the enterprise.

2. The business perspective is an insightful way to link IM&M to the business. IM&M exists to enable the best possible solutions to business practices. It has no intrinsic value. The value of computing lies in applications—how computing is applied—not in microprocessors, storage devices, etc.

3. The technologist perspective offers accidental value to the enterprise.

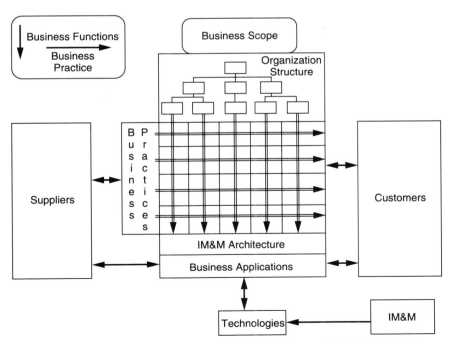

Figure 2.6 Revised management perspective of the business and IM&M.

4. Since client/server computing is a "powerful" architecture (to be proven in Chap. 7, "Client/Server Computing"), it needs to be positioned as the foundation/framework of the business application portfolio. This is to permit the inheritance of the "powerful" architecture attributes to the applications. This is of such critical importance to the long-term competitive viability of the enterprise that it merits being undertaken within the strategic management framework.

You cannot win if you pre-position yourself to lose; to the contrary, you must pre-position yourself to win.

3

Business Competition

The purpose of this chapter is to develop a model through which we can assess the competitive health of an enterprise. The normal operating environment for most companies, except those granted a monopoly status, is that of competition. Their health depends to a large degree on their ability to develop, sustain, and extend ever more competitive advantages. Assets used effectively contribute to corporate competitive health. Assets utilized ineffectively drain and endanger competitive health with the end-game consequences of decline and death of the enterprise.

We will use the Five Forces Model* as the arbiter of corporate competitive health. The Five Forces Model is a well-established and documented analytical methodology for understanding the dynamic interplay of forces that combine to determine the competitive situation and state of an industry. Our agenda for this chapter will be as follows:

- *Section 3.1: Five Forces Model.* We will explain in detail the Five Forces Model.

- *Section 3.2: Business in the 1990s.* We will examine the major business issues that can be anticipated as having a major impact on business actions in the 1990s. We will then integrate the Five Forces Model, the major business issues of the 1990s, and the Strategic Planning Model to understand the importance of "maneuverability" to the competitive health of the enterprise.

The derived model from this chapter will be used in Chap. 6, "The Business Problem," to measure the degree of illness that IM&M

---

* This presentation is a variation of "How Competitive Forces Shape Competition," Michael Porter, *HBR*, March/April 1979.

pathology imposes on the enterprise, and in Chap. 7, "Client/Server Computing," to understand how client/server computing treats the business problems and can dramatically improve the corporation's competitive positioning and health.

3.1   Five Forces Model

The Five Forces Model asserts that the state of competition in an industry is a function of the dynamic interplay of five forces:

- *Supplier Power.*   The power of the industry suppliers to control prices, quality, and overall conditions of purchase of goods and services.

- *Buyer/Customer Power.*   The power of the customers of an industry to exploit their position to influence prices, quality, and overall conditions of purchase of goods and services.

- *Threat of Entry.*   The degree of probability that new competitors will enter the marketplace.

- *Substitute Products.*   The availability and attractiveness of substitute products to the buyers.

- *Rivalry of Existing Competitors.*   The intensity of "jockeying for position" among the incumbent competitors.

The collective position of an enterprise relative to the Five Forces at any time determines its competitive health. Initiatives which improve position in any of the dimensions improve corporate health. Problems which retard or constrain the ability of the enterprise to deal effectively with an adverse force undermine corporate health. Corporate health from this perspective equates to the ability of the corporation to compete by virtue of its state or position relative to each of the Five Forces.

Figure 3.1 illustrates the relationship of the enterprise to the Five Forces. The enterprise is in a constant battle to improve or at least maintain its overall competitive position. To do this, it will undertake initiatives to improve its position with respect to some force. Likewise, at any time, it will react to the initiatives of others who are trying to improve their position at the enterprise's expense. At any given time, thousands of actions and reactions will be going on simultaneously as the industry players endlessly maneuver to improve position.

Each of the Five Forces will now be explained in more detail:

- *Supplier Power.*   Supplier Power is the degree to which suppliers can determine the conditions of purchase including pricing, quality, and services. Suppliers are powerful when:

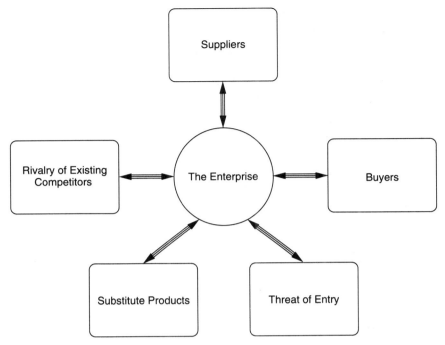

Figure 3.1 Five Forces Model.

Factor	Definition
1. Concentration of suppliers	There is a small and concentrated group of suppliers from whom the customers can buy.
2. Product differentiation	The product is highly differentiated to the point of being proprietary.
3. Switching costs	The buyer would experience enormous expense to change suppliers. Switching costs should be interpreted liberally to include time, labor, disruption of service, retraining, etc.
4. Substitute products	There exist few if any substitute products offering equal/superior feature/functionality on better terms.
5. Customer bypass	The supplier can bypass the customer and sell directly to the customer's customer.
6. Customer importance	The supplier has a diversified set of customers, none of which can individually, markedly, and/or negatively impact his or her business.

The competitive health of an enterprise compared with its suppliers, at the extreme, is then as follows:

Factor	Strong competitive health	Poor competitive health
1. Concentration of suppliers	Many suppliers	Few suppliers/ monopoly supplier
2. Product differentiation	Product is commodity	Product is proprietary
3. Switching costs	Low	High
4. Substitute products	Many	Few/none
5. Customer bypass	Not possible	Easily done
6. Customer importance	Very important	Unimportant

- *Buyer/Customer Power.* Buyer Power is the degree to which the buyer's ability to influence price, quality, and other terms of purchase gives the buyer an advantageous bargaining position. Buyers are powerful when:

Factor	Definition
1. Buyer concentration	The buyer is a large volume purchaser—particularly when the supplier has high fixed costs or a perishable product.
2. Product is commodity	The product is a commodity and easily acquired elsewhere.
3. Product as component of buyer's cost structure	The product is a high or relatively highest part of the buyer's cost structure for his or her product.
4. Buyer's profitability	The profitability of the buyer is marginal and the buyer has a strong motivation to cut/control costs.
5. Product's importance to buyer	The product is not important to the quality, feature/functionality, or differentiation of the buyer's product.
6. Product is viewed as an expense	The product is viewed as an expense by the buyer. It is neither viewed as a way to save money nor is it viewed as adding value. It is simply a necessary but undesired cost.
7. Supplier bypass	The buyer can either bypass the supplier and purchase from the supplier's supplier or do it themselves.

The competitive health of an enterprise relative to its customers is, at the extreme, as follows:

Factor	Strong competitive health	Poor competitive health
1. Buyer concentration	Diversified group of customers	One customer
2. Product is commodity	Differentiated product	Commodity product
3. Product as component of buyer's cost structure	Low percent of cost	High percentage or primary cost component
4. Buyer's profitability	Highly profitable	Marginally profitable
5. Product's importance to customer	Product is critical to customer's product	Product function is viewed as required
6. Product is viewed as an expense	Product saves customer money and/or adds unique value	Product is an expense
7. Supplier bypass	Buyer cannot bypass	Buyer can bypass

■ *Threat of Entry.* Threat of Entry is the degree to which there is a viable probability that new entrants will join in selling to the marketplace and in doing so increase competition for market share. Barriers to entry are as follows:

Factor	Definition
1. Economies of scale	The costs associated with achieving the necessary economies of scale to achieve competitive pricing.
2. Product differentiation	The differentiation of incumbent products which have earned high customer loyalty.
3. Customer switching costs	The total cost of switching products which will deter changing suppliers.
4. Capital requirements	The degree of up-front investment required to enter the marketplace.
5. Non-economy-of-scale advantages	Non-economy-of-scale advantages which the incumbents enjoy, such as patents, special skills, location, learning curve experience, etc.

6. Distribution chan-
nel access
: The ability to get existing distributors to sell product or build a new distribution channel.

7. Government policy
: The degree to which government policies and laws control entry into a market.

8. Retaliation of incumbents
: The degree to which the incumbents have demonstrated that they will strongly defend their markets from new entrants.

The competitive health of an enterprise with respect to the Threat of Entry is, at the extreme, as follows:

Factor	Strong competitive health	Poor competitive health
1. Economies of scale	Large volume required	Small volumes adequate to price competitively
2. Product differentiation	Differentiated product	Commodity product
3. Customer switching costs	High	Low
4. Capital requirements	High	Low
5. Non-economy-of-scale advantages	Many	Few
6. Distribution channel access	Blocked	Open
7. Government policy	Block new entrants	Underwrites new entrants
8. Retaliation of incumbents	Strong retaliation record and capability	No retaliation history or capability

- *Substitute Products.* Substitute Products constrain the ability of an enterprise to control the pricing, quality, and other factors of sale since the customer at some point may switch. Substitute products become important when:

Factor	Definition
1. Strong substitute	The substitutes are a strong feature/functionality clone.
2. Substitute price/performance trend	The substitute is experiencing better price performance improvement than the product for which it substitutes.

3. Profitability of substitute product industry	The substitute product industry is enjoying strong profitability and is looking for new markets in which to grow.
4. Competitive rivalry of substitute product industry	The strong competitive nature of the substitute product industry motivates suppliers to look for easier battlefields.

The competitive health of an enterprise with respect to the threat of substitute products is, at the extreme, as follows:

Factor	Strong competitive health	Poor competitive health
1. Strong substitute	No	Yes
2. Substitute price/performance	Lower than product	Higher than product
3. Profitability of substitute product industry	Low	High
4. Competitive rivalry of substitute product industry	Low	High

- *Rivalry of Existing Competitors.* Rivalry is the degree to which existing competitors battle for market share. The degree of rivalry is a function of the following factors:

Factor	Definition
1. Number and equality of competitors	The number of competitors and the equality of their size.
2. Market growth	The anticipated industry growth (or lack of growth).
3. Product differentiation	The degree to which products by competitors are substitutes for each other.
4. Customer switching costs	The expense a customer incurs in changing suppliers.
5. Fixed costs	The degree of fixed costs a competitor has and/or the perishability of the product.
6. Unit of capacity increment	The amount of additional product produced per investment in unit capacity increase.
7. Exit barriers	Assets, loyalty, commitment, etc. by a competitor to the market.

8. Diversity of corpo-   The degree to which different corporate
rate personalities   personalities, shared values, etc. cause the
combatants to "bump" into each other.

The competitive health of an enterprise relative to competitor rivalry is, at the extreme, as follows:

Factor	Strong competitive health	Poor competitive health
1. Number and equality of competitors	Few and smaller	Many and bigger
2. Market growth	High	Low or negative
3. Product differentiation	Product highly differentiated	Commodity product
4. Customer switching costs	High	Low
5. Fixed costs	Low	High
6. Unit of capacity increment	Low	High
7. Exit barriers	Few	Many
8. Diversity of corporate personalities	Same	Different

Figure 3.2 will be used later in Chap. 6, "The Business Problem," to illustrate the effect that IM&M problems have on the competitive health of the enterprise. The qualitative measures on the graph are as follows:

- *Weakens competitive health.* The IM&M problem retards, drags, disables and/or restricts competitive capability.

- *Neutral.* The IM&M problem does not impact the ability to act or react vis-à-vis that factor.

- *Strengthens competitive health.* The IM&M problem improves the ability of the enterprise to act or react to competitive threats (highly unlikely).

Table 3.1 summarizes the Five Forces and their decomposed factors. With this basic understanding of the Five Forces Model, we can understand how to assess competitive corporate health. At any given time, the Five Forces will be impacting on the enterprise as follows:

1. *No impact:* A Five Force factor is dormant.

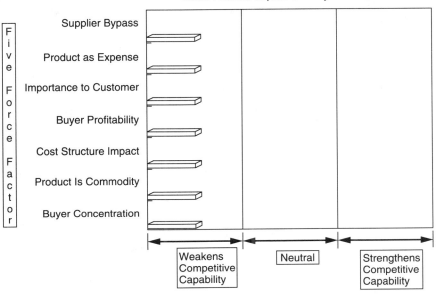

IM&M Problem Impact On "Buyer" Five Force

Figure 3.2   Five Forces Impact Graph.

2. *An act by another:* A supplier, customer, rival, etc., takes an action to improve his or her position at your expense. It is necessary to react promptly or potentially lose market share.

3. *An act by the enterprise:* The enterprise initiates an act to improve its competitive position through the Five Forces at the expense of a supplier, customer, competitor, potential competitor, etc.

4. *External act:* An event occurs outside the Five Forces Model (war, power failure, economic swing, etc.) that requires a response by the enterprise.

At any given time, there are a multitude of actions occurring that require the enterprise to be able to "maneuver." It must be able to "act" (attempt to reposition itself about the Five Forces at somebody else's expense) or "react" (to defend itself from the initiatives of others who are trying to reposition themselves at the enterprise's expense). In either case, there is an urgent need for swift and agile mobility to deal with the "warfare."

Normally, the degree to which IM&M problems hurt the enterprise is expressed in terms of:

- *Cost disadvantage:* The degree to which IM&M failure raises expenses or prevents realization of profitable opportunities.

TABLE 3.1   The Five Forces

The Competitive Health of an Enterprise Is a Function of Its Position with Respect to All of the Five Forces and the Associated Factors

Five Force	Five Force factor	Strong competitive health	Weak competitive health
Supplier	Concentration of suppliers	Many	Few
	Product differentiation	Commodity	Proprietary
	Switching costs	Low	High
	Substitute products	Many	Few
	Customer bypass	Not possible	Easily done
	Customer importance	Very	Unimportant
Buyer	Concentration of buyers	Diversified	One customer
	Product is commodity	Differentiated	Commodity
	Product as component of buyer's cost structure	Low percent	High percent
	Buyers profitability	High	Low/marginal
	Importance of product	Critical	Required
	Product viewed as an expense	Saves customer money	Expense
	Supplier bypass	Cannot	Can
Threat of entry	Economies of scale	Large volume	Small volumes
	Product differentiation	Differentiated	Commodity
	Switching costs	High	Low
	Capital requirements	High	Low
	Non-economy-of-scale advantages	Many	Few
	Distribution channel access	Blocked	Open
	Government policy	Block new entrants	Underwrite new
	Retaliation of incumbents	Strong record	No retaliation history
Substitute products	Strong substitute	No	Yes
	Substitute price/performance	Lower than product	Higher than product
	Profitability of substitute product industry	Low	High
	Competitor rivalry	Low	High
Competitor rivalry	Number and equality of competitors	Few and smaller	
	Market growth	High	Low
	Product differentiation	Differentiated	Commodity
	Switching costs	High	Low
	Fixed costs	Low	High
	Unit of capacity increment	Low	High
	Exit barriers	Few	Many
	Diversity of corporate personalities	Same	Different

- *Time disadvantage:*   The degree to which IM&M failure elongates the time to market, time to service, time to respond, etc.

- *Feature/function disadvantage:*   The degree to which IM&M failure prevents adding value to a product or service.

While this is initially helpful, it is obvious and not terribly insightful. What the Five Forces Model really tells us is the competitive primacy of the ability to maneuver. As valuable as they are, customer loyalty, differentiation, price advantage, location, head start, etc. are all transitory advantages that will undergo constant attack. True advantage lies in the ability to adapt, to act and react as called for (i.e., to be able to maneuver constantly against the Five Forces). The only advantage that you can develop and perfect that is beyond your competitors' ability to take from you is your innate ability to maneuver, change, and adapt.

By implication of this analysis, the Five Forces Model instructs us in the attributes of a "powerful" IM&M architecture. If the essence of competitive advantage is maneuverability to deal proactively and reactively with the Five Forces, then a powerful IM&M architecture must have the following attributes:

- *Maintainability.*   The ease of maintaining the architecture.

- *Modularity.*   The ability to add, modify, and remove pieces of the architecture.

- *Scalability.*   The ability to scale the architecture by the dimensions of transaction volume, data storage volume, concurrent users, and/or total users.

- *Adaptability.*   The ease of change.

- *Portability.*   The ability to move applications in whole or in part across the architecture.

- *Openness/support for standards.*   The compliance of the architecture with open standards that enables many other attributes.

- *Flexibility.*   The ability to grow and contract the architecture as required.

- *Autonomy.*   The ability to function both individually and as part of the whole.

- *Data accessibility.*   The ability to access data both local and remotely transparent to its location.

- *Interoperability.*   The ability to move transactions and data cooperatively across heterogeneous environments.

- *Appliance (user interface device) connectivity.*   The ability for a wide variety of appliances to attach to the architecture.

These architecture attributes sum to the attribute of *maneuverability*. Maneuverability is the prime requirement that business practices impose on IM&M. We will later demonstrate the following:

- The current problems with the application of IM&M are not due to time, cost, or feature/function disadvantage (though these are clearly symptoms), but due to immobility (the IM&M problems constrain, drag, prevent, retard, etc. the enterprise from acting and reacting).
- Client/server computing enables maneuverability.

The maxim of business strategy is not to rely on competitors not appearing, but to be able to rely on the ability to maneuver in dealing with them.

3.2   Business in the 1990s

The Five Forces Model is a generic model of competitiveness, and at any time different factors will take on a dominant position relative to the others. To what extent will maneuverability remain critical in the 1990s? Will the business environment exaggerate its importance or downplay it? Is agility, adaptability, and flexibility the inherent capability we need to nourish to be successful in this decade?

As the 1990s progress, it would appear that agility will be more required than ever. The following is a partial list of the major predictable issues which will impact the enterprise (see Fig. 3.3):

1. *Globalization:* worldwide product development for worldwide markets with worldwide competition.

2. *Demographics:* the aging of the domestic work force and changed distribution of ethnic groups within the work force.

3. *Marketing:* the need to ever more discreetly define and satisfy micromarkets.

4. *Corporate volatility:* mergers, acquisitions, reorganizations, strategic alliances, and bankruptcies.

5. *Technology change:* faster and faster introduction of new products and shorter and shorter life cycles of existing products.

6. *Cost control:* fundamental and relentless pressure to control costs.

7. *The consumer:* a customer more demanding, quality conscious, and service-oriented.

8. *Education:* the decline in the quality of the graduates of the education system.

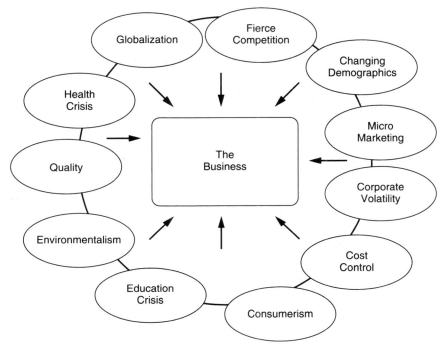

Figure 3.3   Strategic Planning Model II.

9. *Environmentalism:* concern for the environment, with impact on expansion, natural resource availability, and public perception of the good corporate citizen.

10. *Financial markets:* interest rate volatility and savings industry bail-out.

11. *Political change:* arrival of the European market, collapse of the Soviet empire and continued tension in the Middle East.

12. *Productivity:* continued pressure to improve output per unit of input.

13. *Quality:* Demming and Baldrige standards as minimum capabilities.

14. *Health crisis:* The exponential rise in health costs.

Of course, these are only the issues that are currently knowable. Nobody can foretell what other issues will emerge and take on dominance during the decade.

Every game of chance (gambling) has an ante. If you're going to sit at the table, you must know the rules of the game, the stakes you're playing for, and the ante required to play the game. In the 1990s, the stake is enterprise prosperity; the rules of the game are subject to all these changes (as well as numerous ones that are unforeseeable); and the "ante" is maneuverability.

Figure 3.4 revises the previously introduced strategic planning model to show the importance of the Five Forces Model on the entire planning and implementation process. As the Five Forces, exaggerated by all the issues just itemized, impact the strategy process, it will be more important than ever that business strategies are able to be maneuvered, recast, and adapted as required to deal with the constantly changing situation. The business needs to be able to maneuver its IM&M whenever and however required. The IM&M asset should never be a constraint on business actions.

> . . . The ability to gain victory by changing and adapting according to the opponent is called genius.*

3.3 Conclusions

The contribution to building sustainable competitive advantages that business requires of the Information Movement and Management resource is the ability to continually maneuver in response to the competitive Five Forces. The only lasting competitive advantage is the ability to continually adapt to change in response to "whatever." The business requires freedom of movement.

The freedom to maneuver provided by an architecture can be expressed in terms of "reach and range"† (see Fig. 3.5). *Reach* defines to whom you can connect. *Range* defines what information and services can be shared. The more complete the reach and range of the architecture, the greater the freedom of maneuverability, the greater the adaptability of the enterprise to change, the greater the ability to act and react, and the greater the competitive advantage.

The business issues of the 1990s (see Fig. 3.4) are accelerating the mean time to obsolescence of business applications. Positioning oneself to be able to continuously adapt is not only an issue of competitive advantage, it is an issue of competitive necessity as well. In future chapters, we will learn how client/server computing meets this necessity and, in fact, expands both our reach and range.

---

* *The Art of War* by Sun Tzu.
† The material on reach and range is adopted from *Shaping the Future,* P. Keen, Harvard Business School Press, 1991.

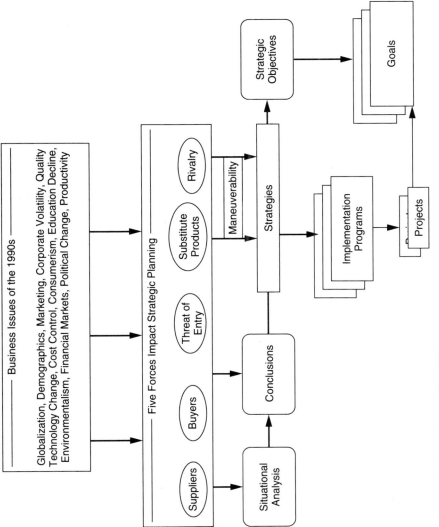

Figure 3.4 Business issues of the 1990s.

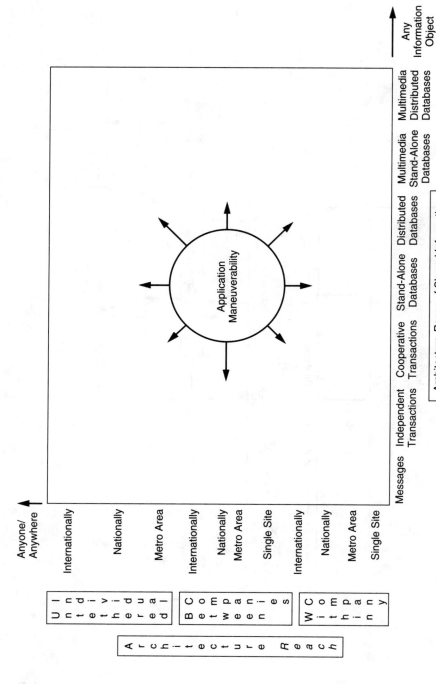

Figure 3.5 Reach and range.

4

IM&M Architecture

The purpose of this chapter is to develop a much better understanding of systems architecture. In the opening chapter, it was asserted that many problems experienced by the business application portfolio were rooted in a weak architecture. It was also suggested that a powerful architecture was strategically important to the enterprise since it positions the applications advantageously; the application's portfolio is inherently better able to deal with the continuing change inflicted by the dynamic marketplace and all the competitive forces. Since the notion of a powerful architecture is basic to the book's thesis, it is necessary to assure a shared understanding of what is meant when we discuss architecture. To accomplish this, the material in this chapter will be presented as follows:

- *Section 4.1: Business Applications.* This section will develop a better understanding of the nature of business applications. Applications bind business practices to architecture.

- *Section 4.2: Data Architecture.* This section will develop an optimum data architecture for the enterprise.

- *Section 4.3: Processing Architecture.* This section will develop an understanding of the different processing architectures available upon which to construct the applications portfolio.

- *Section 4.4: A Powerful Architecture.* This section will synthesize a powerful architecture for the building of business applications to achieve current competitive advantage and be adaptable for future competitive advantage.

Architecture is the underlying cause of many problems which preempt the effective use of IM&M by the enterprise. Its study must not be ignored.

4.1   Business Applications

As was illustrated in Fig. 2.2, "Management Perspective of IM&M and the Business," and Fig. 2.5, "Revised Management Perspective of IM&M and the Business," the business practices of the enterprise are automated in the form of business applications that collectively compose the business systems portfolio. Companies have innumerable practices requiring IM&M capability. Typical applications would include:

- Order realization
- Customer service
- Contract administration
- Product development
- Benefits administration
- Staffing
- Budget development and monitoring
- Information sharing (E-mail, conferencing, team support, etc.)

The list is endless.

As illustrated in Fig. 4.1, the business practices can generally be partitioned into two broad classifications:

- *The Business Applications.*   Those business applications that operationally "run" the business on a daily, weekly, monthly, etc. basis. When they cease to run, the business literally stops operating.

- *The About-the-Business Applications.*   Those applications that analyze the business. They aid both in interpreting what has occurred and deciding prudent actions for the future. When they cease to run, there is no immediately obvious business failure, but their utility is critical to the long-term competitiveness of the enterprise.

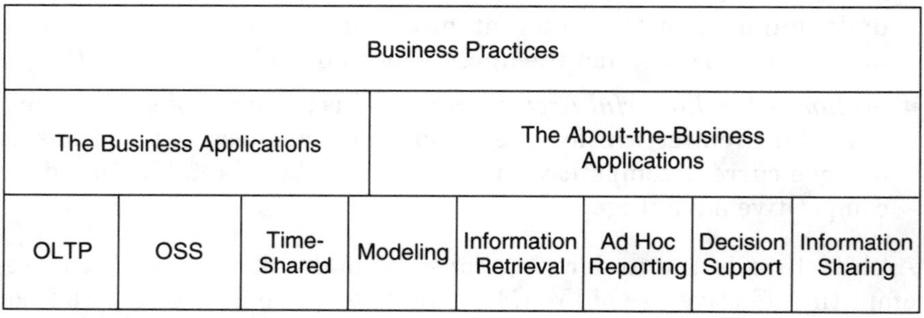

Business Practices								
The Business Applications				The About-the-Business Applications				
OLTP	OSS	Time-Shared	Modeling	Information Retrieval	Ad Hoc Reporting	Decision Support	Information Sharing

Figure 4.1   Application models.

The Business Applications are often called *On-Line Transaction Processing Systems* (OLTP) or *Operations Support Systems* (OSS) and have the following general attributes:

1. They are heavy-duty production transaction record-keeping systems that directly support the execution of a business practice.

2. They may have to provide 24-hour by 7-day service and have carefully managed outage periods.

3. Database integrity and availability are crucial. The database must be recoverable from a failure within a guaranteed restoration period.

4. They are performance measurable in terms of transactions/(sub)second and/or user response time (x percent of the transactions must respond in less than y (sub)seconds).

5. They are structured applications with both predefined transactions and predefined transaction flows. The execution paths are predictable.

6. The database schemas are quite complex in terms of number of entities and number of interentity relationships. The interentity relationships impose multiple dependency and validation requirements on the system.

7. Elaborate editing of input transactions is required to ensure and maintain database quality.

8. Security of access is important.

9. Sophisticated dialogue management is required.

10. There is a strong concern for user ergonomics to maximize productivity.

11. There are often large applications by the metrics of database size, total number of users, total number of concurrent users, and types of transactions.

12. There is extensive off-prime-time batch updating and reporting that must be completed within a tight batch window.

The payoff advantage from these types of applications is in maximizing the efficiency of the business. Consequently, they will often contain exception-monitoring subsystems used to advise management when an abnormal situation has occurred or an undesirable pattern is developing.

The About-the-Business Applications are often called *Information Center Applications* (decision support, modeling, information retrieval, ad hoc reporting/analysis, what-if, etc.). This class of applications is retrieval/analysis/report/information-sharing-oriented. The data sources are often triggered extracts from OLTP or OSS applications or information services. These applications have the following attributes.

1. Static (low-update) databases

2. Periodic refreshing of the database from the source OLTP or OSS application

3. Extended time accumulation of data

4. Simple restore/recovery

5. Facilities to enable the "canning" of repetitive user requests

6. Flexible import/export facilities

7. Enable sharing of information

8. An analyst workbench that may include:

  - graphics
  - report writers
  - statistical modeling
  - spreadsheets
  - simulators
  - query languages
  - word processors
  - desktop publishing
  - project management software

The payoff from this class of applications is better knowledge about the business.

Applications are often continuous in capability and their functionality may not be discrete. Though an application will normally migrate to one classification as its primary definer, it may have subsystems that are more aligned to the other type. Both the Business Applications and the About-the-Business Applications with all the endless variations are built on top of a *data architecture* and a *processing architecture* that jointly compose the *IM&M architecture* for the business. A complete IM&M architecture would also include a set of standards and management IM&M practices.

4.2   Data Architecture

Business applications are performed by programs that collect, create, modify, retrieve, and delete data and programs that use, analyze, summarize, extract, and/or in other ways manipulate data. Data is the common thread that ties together the extensive corporate application portfolio. Data, transformed into information as it flows between users, can provide current advantage in the form of superior operational systems, and future advantage in the form of superior analysis for planning. How the data asset is positioned is of vital long-term importance to the health of the enterprise.

Increasingly, corporations are recognizing that the purposeful management and leveraging of the corporate data asset must take on increased attention in the 1990s. In the 1970s, management attention was focused on hardware cost. During the 1980s, management's attention shifted to software as both a growing element of the IM&M cost structure and the source of advantageous applications. In the 1990s, management will increasingly focus on data exploitation as the path to improved customer service, cooperation with suppliers, and the creation of new barriers for competitors.

Data engineering theory (*data engineering* is the discipline that studies how to model, analyze, and design data for maximum utility) indicates that there are four generic data environments on which to build business applications. For a variety of technical and architectural reasons, they are not equally advantageous. Figure 4.2 illustrates the four options that can be explained as follows:

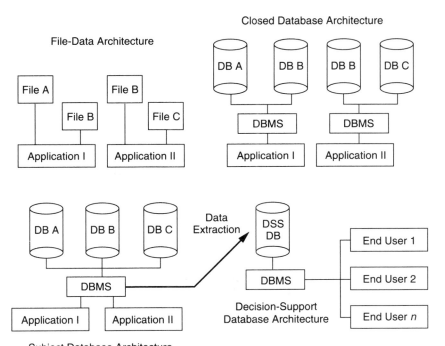

Figure 4.2 Alternative data architectures.

1. *Dedicated file architecture.*   Each application has a set of privately designed files. The data structure is tightly embedded with the application, and the data files are owned by the application.

2. *Closed database architecture.*   A database management system (DBMS) is used to provide technological advantage over file systems (exemplary advantages are views, security, atomicity, locking, recovery, etc.), but distinct, separate, and independent databases are still designed for each application. The DBMS is used as a private and powerful file system with the data remaining the proprietary property of the application. As is true with the dedicated file architecture, there is a high degree of data redundancy and frequently poor data administration. Spaghetti-like interfaces move data between the closed databases. Since these interfaces often have to convert, edit, and/or restructure data as it moves between proprietary definitions, they are often called *data scrubbers* or translators. Data scrubbers do not add value; they compensate for inadequate data administration.

3. *Subject database architecture.*   Data is analyzed, modeled, structured, and stored based on its own internal attributes, independent of any specific application. Data is administered as a shareable resource through a data administration function that owns the data for all potential users. Extensive sharing of data occurs through application-sensitive views. Subject databases run the day-to-day operations of the enterprise.

4. *Decision-support database architecture.*   Databases are constructed for quick searching retrieval, ad hoc queries, and ease of use. The data is normally a periodic extract from a subject database. To minimize the number of extracts and to insure time/content-consistent data, data is shared at the corporate, departmental, and local levels (not extracted per user). Data definitions are maintained in synchronization with the source databases to insure the ability to interrelate data from multiple subject database extracts without the need to resort to data scrubbers. Decision-support databases are used to analyze the enterprise.

The recommended data architecture is a mixture of the subject database and decision-support database environments: subject databases to support the Business Applications and decision-support databases to enable the About-the-Business applications. This dual database architecture is most advantageous for the following reasons:

1. It maximizes data quality.

2. It maximizes data accessibility.

3. It maximizes data sharing.

4. It eliminates unplanned-for data redundancy.

5. It simplifies interapplication interaction.

6. It assures data standardization.

7. It maximizes application life-cycle productivity.

8. It accelerates the development of new applications that can reuse the in-place data resource.

9. It enables the creation of centers of excellence in data management to protect the data asset.

Figure 4.3 illustrates what the optimum data architecture would look like. It merges the subject database and decision-support database environment together. Notice that data moves down from corporate to departmental to local decision-support databases to minimize extraction.

Some data architects would prefer a single database environment where both OLTP and decision-support needs are fulfilled concurrently against a single database, and thereby eliminate duplication and extract altogether. It is our assessment that the two user communities have fundamentally different and incompatible requirements that preclude this ideal option. Table 4.1 summarizes the major points of conflict. These dichotomies present a formidable barrier to a single database environment.

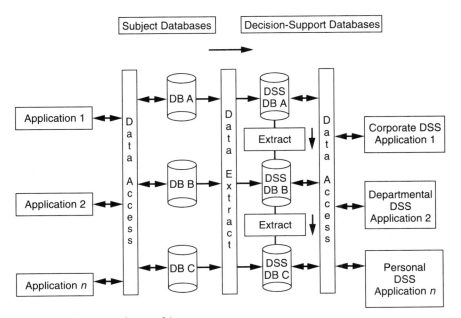

Figure 4.3 Corporate data architecture.

TABLE 4.1   Dichotomy between Operational and Decision-Support Environments

The Operational and the Decision-Support Environment Have Different Attributes

Operational environment: Subject Databases The Business Applications	Decision-Support environment: Decision-Support Databases The About-the-Business Applications
Stores very detailed data	Stores detailed and/or summarized data
Stores entire subject database	Stores only data of interest
Requires to-the-last-transaction accuracy	Requires "as of" accuracy
Disciplined and highly structured planned transactions	Unstructured and ad hoc transactions
Optimized for performance, efficiency, and availability	Optimized for flexibility and ease of use
Maintains rigorous data structures	Supports dynamic data structures
Runs the business	Analyzes the business
Emphasizes needs of all potential users	Emphasizes needs of each user
Short-running and engineered transactions	Potentially long-running and dynamically defined transactions

When routine access is given to operational databases by decision-support users, experience suggests the following major problems occur.

1. *Performance.*   The unpredictable nature of the ad hoc queries disrupts the requirement of predictable response time for operational systems. Predictable and guaranteed performance cannot be engineered into the system design if the transactions are not predictable.

2. *Data retention.*   The decision-support applications often require retention of data longer for cumulative analysis than the operational systems that only need it for the active business-practice cycle. The growth in the size of the database can negatively impact performance, integrity, and the ability to meet any recoverability time constraints.

3. *Logical reasoning.*   Since the database is dynamically changing with each transaction, information queries are nonrepeatable, and chained queries do not necessarily operate on the same set of data. Deductive reasoning against a stable data store is not feasible. A temporal database that maintains a time view of the data could resolve this problem, but creates a new set of issues unrelated to the pressing operational needs.

We may summarize our views on data architecture as follows:

- There are four generic ways to design and organize the corporation's data asset.
- They are not equal.
- A combination of the subject database and decision-support database environments is most advantageous.

- A single database environment from which both operational and decision-support requirements are met is desirable but plagued by many practical problems that make it infeasible.

Now that we understand how to position the data by decoupling it from applications and positioning it as a shareable resource, how do we best design the processing architecture to access it?

4.3   Processing Architecture

The processing architecture defines the framework upon which applications are designed and implemented. The programs that compose an application generally perform three core functions:

- *Presentation services.*   The interface between the program and the external environment.

- *Processing/algorithmic services.*   The execution of the logic of the business practice.

- *Data manipulation services.*   The addition, modification, retrieval, and deletion of records in the data store. This includes the associated record manipulation logic.

There does not exist an equivalent theory for processing architecture selection as there does for data architecture. Nevertheless, through observation and experience, a few general architectures have ascended to a dominant presence. Systems, subsystems, and supersystems are constructed by linking together instances of each architecture (and endless variations) into a final application architecture.

We will now analyze ten common processing architectures with their associated key attributes. To help distinguish them, the associated illustration will highlight where presentation processing and data services occur within the architecture. The most pervasive processing architectures are as follows:

1. *Host OLTP architecture (Fig. 4.4).*   This is a specific instance of the host-centered computing architecture" (Fig. 1.2). It is the historical preeminent platform for running the Business Applications. Common attributes of this architecture are as follows:

   - dumb-terminal (asynchronous or synchronous) user access
   - a teleprocessing monitor to manage transaction flow
   - a DBMS to manage the data
   - a glass house mainframe environment, a minicomputer, or a specialized computer such as a fault-tolerant processor to ensure continuous operations
   - programming done in a combination of third-generation (COBOL) and fourth-generation languages

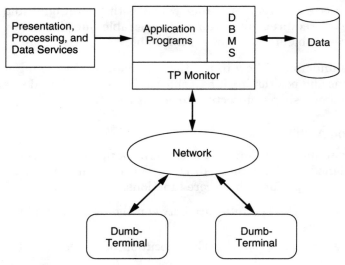

Figure 4.4   Host OLTP architecture.

2. *Host batch architecture (Fig. 4.5).*   This is a specific instance of the host-centered computing architecture (Fig. 1.2), but without the interactive terminal capability. It provides a platform for running large (large means long-running) batch programs for either the Business Applications or the About-the-Business Applications. Common attributes of this environment are as follows:

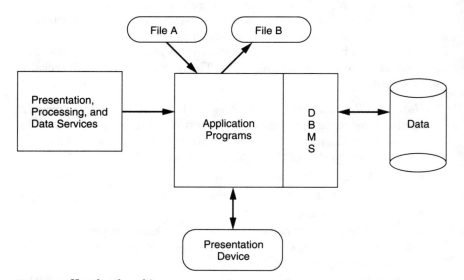

Figure 4.5   Host-batch architecture.

- noninteractive by definition
- third-generation programming languages
- report writers
- file system intensive
- a DBMS to manage the data
- mainframe and minicomputer (background) based
- job control software management

Sometimes, batch programs run simultaneously with OLTP applications and have batch access to the teleprocessing monitor.

3. *Time-sharing architecture (Fig. 4.6).* This is also a specific instance of the host-centered computing architecture (Fig. 1.2). It provides a platform for application development, end-user computing, running About-the-Business applications and departmental record-keeping and administration systems. Generally, DBMS integrity requirements, volumes of data, number of users, and guaranteed response time is not as stringent as is customary in the OLTP environment. Common attributes of this environment are as follows:

- end-user tools
- a DBMS to manage the data

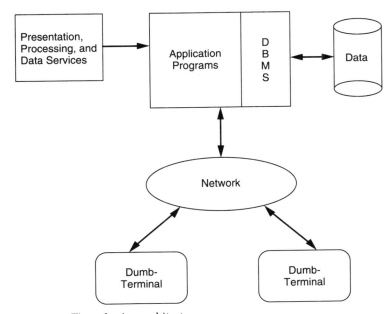

Figure 4.6   Time-sharing architecture.

- third-generation, fourth-generation, and special purpose languages
- often minicomputer based

4. *Terminal-emulation architecture (Fig. 4.7).*   This architecture is used to permit two architectures to work together by one processor pretending to be (acting as) a dumb-terminal. The client machine mimics through software the behavior of a terminal that allows an application program to create and receive "screens" (or another terminal device). This architecture is often used to allow departmental processors to interface with mainframes in the absence of a proper peer-to-peer protocol environment. A typical configuration is an OLTP architecture being accessed through terminal emulation by a time-sharing architecture.

5. *File/peripheral server architecture (Fig. 4.8).*   This architecture is used to allow a file or a peripheral (printer, plotter, etc.) on a local area network (LAN) to be shared by multiple processors on the network. While detached and remote, the file/peripheral acts as though it was directly attached to the processor.

   While this permits sharing, the division of labor between processors is not well divided and the result is an inherently inefficient architecture for applications of any volume.

6. *File transfer architecture (Fig. 4.9).*   This architecture is used to permit bulk transfer of large files between processors. A typical scenario is as follows:

   a. An extract is run on processor A to extract required data from an A-owned database.

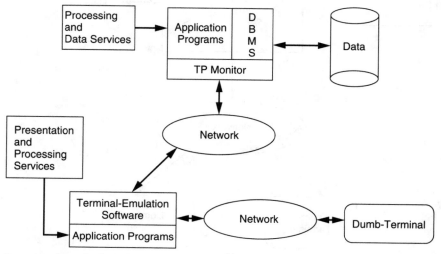

Figure 4.7   Terminal emulation architecture.

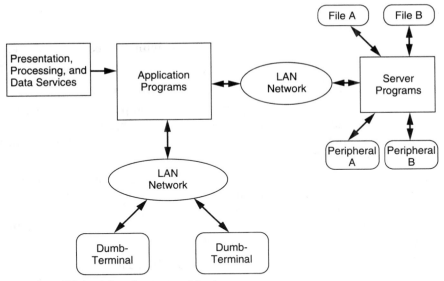

Figure 4.8 File/peripheral server architecture.

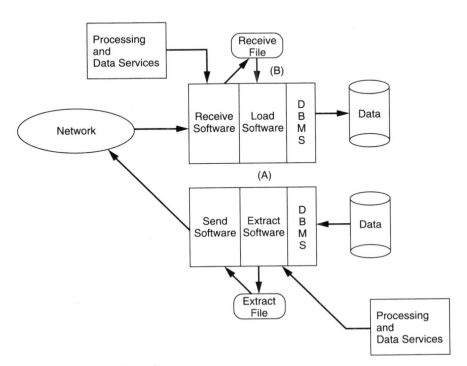

Figure 4.9 File transfer architecture.

    b. The file transfer software sends the file to the receiving processor by communicating with receive software on processor B.

    c. The received file is loaded into the receiving processor database.

Any combination of processors may be involved in file transfer.

7. *Personal computing architecture (Fig. 4.10).* This is the basic architecture that is used to permit personal computing. It is the low-end version of the host-centered computing architecture (Fig. 1.2). Typical applications done on this architecture are word processing, spreadsheets, presentations, and project management.

8. *Cooperative processing architecture (Fig. 4.11).* This architecture is used to permit programs on two architectures to interact dynamically (have a step-by-step conversation) with each other. A specific cooperative processing protocol such as LU 6.2 or TCP-IP is used to define the conversation syntax and rules.

9. *Message-switching architecture (Fig. 4.12).* This architecture is used to permit the routing of formatted messages between processors. Generally a "named" message is put on a queue and the switching software, via established routing tables, knows the location in the network of the program and processor that should receive the message. This architecture is generally used in host OLTP environments.

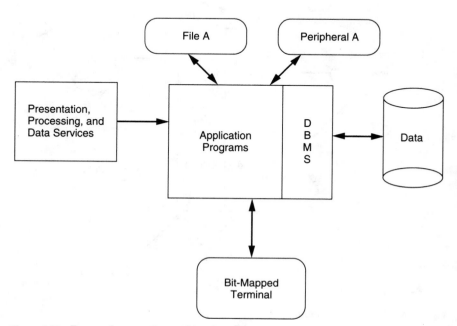

Figure 4.10 Personal computing architecture.

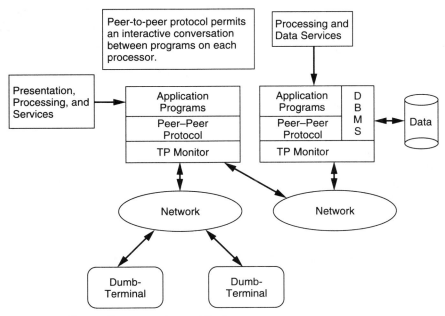

Figure 4.11 Cooperative processing architecture.

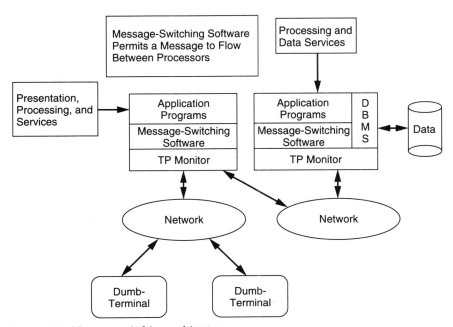

Figure 4.12 Message-switching architecture.

10. *Client/server computing architecture (Fig. 4.13).*   This architecture is used to permit programs on two processors to cooperate transparently to complete a transaction as a single, unified task. Bonding software is built on top of a cooperative processing foundation and operates in the sequence of request, service performed, and reply, as opposed to a meticulous step-by-step conversation (though it logically can be reduced to that).

As was stated before, actual application architectures are built by cutting and pasting these building blocks together in endless permutations.

Though each architecture offers particular benefits in certain situations, some are clearly better than others. Table 4.2 restates the architecture attributes that make an architecture generically better or more powerful. These attributes, as you may recall, were derived from the analysis of the Five Forces Model in Chap. 3. The summation of the attributes is maneuverability. The architecture inherently enables and positions the business to be able to:

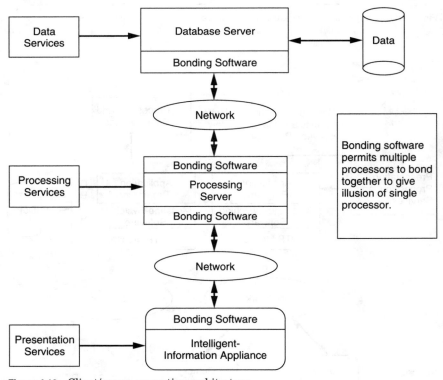

Figure 4.13   Client/server computing architecture.

- *Act*—initiate actions to gain advantage.

- *React*—initiate actions to respond to the acts of others (competitors, suppliers, customers, etc.).

- *Adapt*—maneuver as required according to the dynamics of events.

As decisions are made by management on what actions to take, the applications built on top of a powerful architecture are most easily adapted, since they have inherited the attributes of the architecture. Three of the architecture attributes are particularly important:

- *Data accessibility.* The architecture allows a distributed and increasingly mobile work force to access the shared subject and decision-support databases.

- *Appliance connectivity.* The architecture allows for the easy introduction of a wide variety of appliances from a heterogeneous set of suppliers that allows optimum matching of appliances to business practices. The appliances are also processor-based.

- *Adaptability.* The architecture inherently allows for continual change as the "normal" business situation.

TABLE 4.2   Architecture Attributes

A Powerful Architecture Exhibits These Attributes

Architecture attribute	Definition
Maintainability	The ease of maintaining the architecture
Modularity	The ability to add, modify, and remove pieces of the architecture
Scalability	The ability to scale the architecture by the dimensions of transaction volume, data storage volume, concurrent users, and/or total users
Adaptability	The ease of change
Portability	The ability to move applications across the architecture
Openness/standards	The compliance of the architecture with open standards which enables many of the other attributes
Autonomy	The ability of each part of the architecture to function both independently and as part of the whole
Flexibility	The ability to grow and contract the architecture as required
Data accessibility	The ability to access decoupled data, both locally and remotely
Interoperability	The ability to work cooperatively between multiple heterogeneous processors
Appliance connectivity	The ability for a wide variety of information appliances to attach to the architecture
Maneuverability	The summation of all the attributes which positions the enterprise to both act and react to the dynamics of the competitive marketplace.

It is our assessment that only the client/server computing architecture meets the power requirements. (The cooperative architecture can also meet it, but it is so complicated to program that for practical purposes few could exploit it.) In Chap. 7, "Client/Server Computing," we will demonstrate in detail why this is true. If you doubt this assessment, simply draw a matrix with each architecture listed as the left column and the "power" attributes across the top. It will quickly become obvious that the other architectures fail.

This should not be all that surprising. Figure 4.14 illustrates how a technology moves from a craft to a science-based professional engineering discipline. As a young discipline, the early IM&M architectural efforts are characteristic of the craft stage. Client/server computing represents the transition to a more commercial stage of development. With more maturity, one should anticipate the formalization and development of the client/server computing taking on the characteristics of the professional engineering stage.

We can summarize our conclusion for this section as follows:

- Applications are built on a foundation of processing architectures that serve as the structural building blocks.

- There exist criteria to judge which architectures are inherently more powerful as the general solution. The criteria originate with the Five Forces Model.

- Most of the architectures that have been in use are characteristic of the craft stage of engineering development.

- Client/server computing offers the best solution.

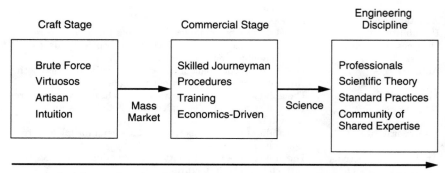

A discipline evolves from being a craft to an engineering discipline over time with the infusion of scientific theory and the need for broad application.

Figure 4.14 Evolution of an engineering discipline.

4.4   A Powerful Architecture

Based on the preceding analysis, it is evident that the optimum IM&M architecture would consist of coupling a subject database/decision-support database environment with the client/server computing architecture. The resulting architecture (illustrated in Fig. 4.15) represents the merging of data architecture with processing architecture. This architecture is often called a *layered* architecture because it naturally lends itself to dividing services into the layers of:

- presentation
- transport
- processing
- data manipulation

It should not be surprising that this is fully congruent with the definition of IM&M given in Chap. 1 and illustrated in Fig. 1.1, "Information Movement and Management Model."

When one melds the layered idea with the architecture attribute of adaptability, it becomes clear why client/server computing is so powerful. Client/server computing is the more general case with the other architectures serving as specific customized and restricted instances.

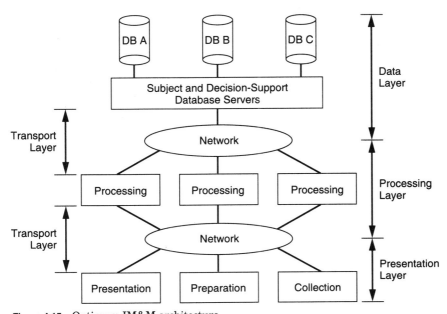

Figure 4.15   Optimum IM&M architecture.

It can, at the extreme, be completely decoupled with presentation, processing, and data manipulation services occurring on different processors connected by local and/or wide area networking, or it can be collapsed with all services occurring on one processor, or a combination of both. It is from these roots that client/server computing enjoys the powers of the others but, simultaneously, enjoys the broader advantages of being the more general case.

The subject database and decision-support database environments have always been desirable but are now for the first time achievable. Coupling of the client/server processing solution with these data environments positions the databases as data servers that can be accessed both locally and remotely. Business-practice-specific appliances can interface to the user and make requests of services from the other layers. Without the client/server architecture, even if you had the foresight and will to attempt to construct a proper data environment, how would your dispersed applications and users have accessed it?

The merging of client/server computing with the subject and decision-support database architectures creates an IM&M architecture that:

- meets the requirements for the optimum data architecture

- meets the requirements for the optimum processing architecture

- meets the requirements of end users for business-practice-specific information appliances

- permits the enterprise to maneuver to meet the needs of the marketplace

- provides the maximum reach and range (see Fig. 3.5) for the business

5

Critical Issues
of Information Systems

The purpose of this chapter is to analyze the critical issues that information system executives have identified as crucial to their enterprises' continual well-being. Annually, leading-edge IM&M consultancies do surveys of Fortune 500 information system executives and chief information officers to determine the critical "to-do" list. The list summarizes the initiatives (acts) that senior information systems management feels must be done to meet corporate objectives.

This list can provide a way complementary to Five Forces analysis to measure the degree of IM&M pathology on the enterprise. Since they surmise the actions needed to be done (by definition), the degree to which IM&M problems inhibit, retard, prevent, or constrain their accomplishment is an alternative measure of the severity of IM&M problems. The degree to which any architecture enables or blocks the achievement of these objectives is another measure of the utility of the architecture.

The remainder of this chapter will present the critical issues in the following format:

- *Issue.* Identifies the issue by title.

- *Definition.* A brief explanation/clarification of the issue.

- *Commentary.* An expansion of the issue, relating it to business strategy and client/server computing.

The list presented is selected from *Critical Issues of Information Systems Management for 1991* by the Index Group and is an excellent representation of the issues. Other lists such as *Top Challenges Facing*

Information Systems Management by Deloitte & Touche Information Technology Consulting Services are equally helpful but, since these types of lists overlap to such a large degree, I have chosen to use one list only.

5.1   Critical Issues Analysis

The following list represents the critical items identified in the 1991 Index Group study. The items are presented in the same order as given in the study. The crucial issues are as follows:

Issue 1:   Reshape business practices through information technology
- *Definition:*   This issue calls for radical business process reengineering with innovative deployment of IM&M as the key aspect of the reengineering. Information technology should/must lead the way to the enterprise of the future.

- *Commentary:*   This issue is motivated by the following factors.

  1. There is growing global competition and the accompanying need to imbue business practices with massive doses of advantage.
  2. The vintage of the embedded base of systems is becoming more and more unresponsive to the changing business climate.
  3. Advantageous technologies to exploit for specific business practices are emerging. Technologies such as portable personal computers, EDI, object-oriented programming and DBMS, imaging, multimedia workstations, and inter-LAN networking are examples of this. There is more than a dumb-terminal, a teleprocessing monitor, a mainframe, and a hierarchical DBMS with which to reengineer.
  4. The arrival of artificial intelligence permits not only process to be automated, but knowledge to be automated as well.

Issue 2:   Aligning corporate and information system goals
- *Definition:*   This issue states that corporate business goals drive IM&M goals, and the two should be in alignment.

- *Commentary:*   This is exactly what was argued in Chap. 2, Sec. 2.2, "The Management Perspective," which asserted that the only purpose of IM&M is to enable the business practices. IM&M has no inherent value unto itself.

Issue 3:   Instituting cross-functional systems
- *Definition:*   This issue recognizes that the business practices cross-functional organization and that effective applications have to service

the business practice across this spectrum. The nature of business practices crossing functional organizations was illustrated in Fig. 2.5, "Revised Management Perspective of the Business and IM&M."

- *Commentary:* This issue recognizes that there is really no such thing as business system*s*. There is really just one continuous and endlessly interconnected business process that by necessity, complexity, technology, practicality, etc., has been partitioned into manageable units (i.e., business applications). It acknowledges the advantage of reuniting selected applications through process and data sharing.

The discussion of data architecture in Chap. 4, Sec. 4.2, "Data Architecture," stated the need to decouple data from applications in order to position it as a shared and reusable resource. Linear applications are integrateable by reusing the same datastore in turn. Similarly, client/server computing permits processors to serve as process servers. Multiple applications can make requests to the same service and thereby ensure common logic and improved productivity through reuse.

Issue 4: Boosting software development productivity

- *Definition:* This issue emphasizes the continual importance of improving software development productivity. Obviously, this is not for its own sake but to enable advantageous applications to be created and enhanced quicker. *Productivity,* in this context, should be viewed as total function delivered per software expense dollar.

Issue 5: Utilizing data

- *Definition:* This issue acknowledges the ascendancy of data as a strategic corporate resource.
- *Commentary:* The shift in management focus from hardware to software to data was discussed in Chap. 4, Sec. 4.2.

Issue 6: Developing an information system strategic plan

- *Definition:* This issue recognizes the importance of a strategic IM&M plan to support the strategic business plan.
- *Commentary:* This issue requires the technology plan to be congruent with the business plan. Again, the business comes first. The most strategic IM&M decision to be made is the putting in place of an IM&M architecture as suggested in Chap. 4, Sec. 4.4, "A Powerful Architecture," which pre-positions the application portfolio for maneuverability. A powerful IM&M architecture would not only support business strategies, but may create the context for new business strategies. As the executive council steers the corporate ship, what

they want from IM&M is the ability to turn the rudder and have the ship respond promptly.

Issue 7: Improving software development quality

- *Definition:* This issue balances Issue 4, "Boosting Software Development Productivity." While Issue 4 is concerned with doing things quickly, this issue is concerned with doing the right things. Both are, of course, required.

- *Commentary:* This issue includes the need to match IM&M technology to the specific requirements of the business practice. One size doesn't fit all, and quality from the user's perspective will be enhanced by technology adjusting to that user and not the reverse.

Issue 8: Creating an information architecture

- *Definition:* This issue recognizes the need to prevent systems entropy (chaos) by constructing the application portfolio within the context of a well-defined and integrated infrastructure consisting of standards, management practices, data architecture, and a processing architecture.

- *Commentary:* Figure 4.15, "Optimum IM&M Architecture," provides the basis for a complete information architecture that requires the melding of appropriate standards and management practices.

Issue 9: Integrating information systems

- *Definition:* This issue recognizes the emerging requirement for interoperability of systems across heterogeneous hardware and software environments.

- *Commentary:* Table 4.2, "Architecture Attributes," summarizes the key attributes required to enable interoperability in its fullest sense.

Issue 10: Improving leadership skills in information systems

- *Definition:* This issue recognizes that, given the penetration of IM&M into the fabric of the business, it is necessary for the IM&M executive community to show leadership in seeing that IM&M is optimally applied.

Issue 11: Cutting information systems costs

- *Definition:* This issue is the continuous concern for maintaining or improving IM&M service while reducing net expenses.

- *Commentary:* If one views *net revenue/IM&M expense* as an important financial measure, this issue reduces to an attempt to improve the measure by denominator management. A visionary approach, which will be required to deal with the business issues of the 1990s discussed in Chap. 3, Sec. 3.2, "Business in the 1990s," would be to not view IM&M as simply a necessary but arduous expense, but rather as a value-added component of the product/service, and to exploit it to accomplish upward numerator management. IM&M should be viewed as an asset, not an expense.

Issue 12: Using information systems for competitive breakthrough

- *Definition:*   This issue is exactly the opposite of Issue 11, "Cutting Information Systems Costs." It extols the use of information systems for radical process/capability improvement. Characteristic of this type of improvement is dramatic and abrupt discontinuous change.

- *Commentary:*   This kind of change markedly redefines the balance of relationships in the Five Forces Model. The most fundamental competitive breakthrough that information systems could accomplish is positioning the enterprise for continuous change through IM&M. While the first wave of computing automated the business, and current actions are under way to reengineer it, competitive breakthrough will provide capabilities to the business designers to "imagineer" the business.

Issue 13: Improving the information system's human resource

- *Definition:*   This issue shows concern for the continued growth and effectiveness of the IM&M staff.

- *Commentary:*   This subject as it relates to client/server computing will be discussed in Chap. 8, "Implementing Client/Server Computing."

Issue 14: Educating management on information systems

- *Definition:*   This issue is concerned with educating senior management in regard to the capabilities that information technology can provide to enable the corporate mission.

- *Commentary:*   Given what will be discussed in Chap. 6, "The Business Problem," this will be a "hard sell."

Issue 15: Connecting to customers and suppliers

- *Definition:*   This issue is concerned with improving business process productivity by electronic bonding (electronic commerce) with customers and suppliers. It recognizes that massive productivity improvements are possible by improving the flow of information to your business partners on each side.

- *Commentary:*   This issue has some very important, but hidden, implications. Figure 2.6, "Revised Management Perspective of the Business and IM&M," illustrated how a powerful IM&M architecture could be the basis of the application portfolio and thereby enable the underlying business practices. Figure 5.1, "Management Perspective of the Business and IM&M Revisited," equates to Fig. 2.6 but magnifies the view of the customer and supplier. There is a great deal of information being passed between the enterprise and the customers and suppliers; everybody's practices are not discrete and separate, but continuous. Figure 5.2, "Customer, Supplier, and the Enterprise as One," illustrates the strategic intent of this issue. By integrating business practices with the customers and suppliers, the following occur:

The artificial barriers to process productivity are broken down.

Improved productivity is gained with suppliers.

Improved service is provided to customers.

The balance of the Five Forces is changed.

Connecting to customers and suppliers permits horizontal economies of scale to be achieved that are mutually beneficial for everyone except new competitors, who have a new barrier to entry. Figure 5.3, "Electronic Commerce," illustrates the productivity opportunities of electronic bonding through EDI (Electronic Data Interchange).

The academic idea being implemented here is called the *value-chain.** The value-chain says that a company imparts value on its products as they move from function to function (the value-chain). By connecting to customers and suppliers, everybody's value-chains can be optimized to mutual benefit.

Issue 16: Managing changes caused by information technology
- *Definition:* This issue recognizes that the introduction of new IM&M technology alters job definitions and traditional work practices. It seeks to preempt problems by anticipating them and including dealing with the displacement issues as part of the technology implementation planning.

Issue 17: Promoting the information systems function
- *Definition:* This issue seeks to keep senior management aware of the contribution that IM&M makes to the business.

Issue 18: Determining the value of information systems
- *Definition:* This issue is concerned with the net cost/benefit of IM&M. It implies that there is concern that the benefit is often lacking.

---

* *Competitive Advantage,* Dr. Michael Porter, The Free Press, 1985.

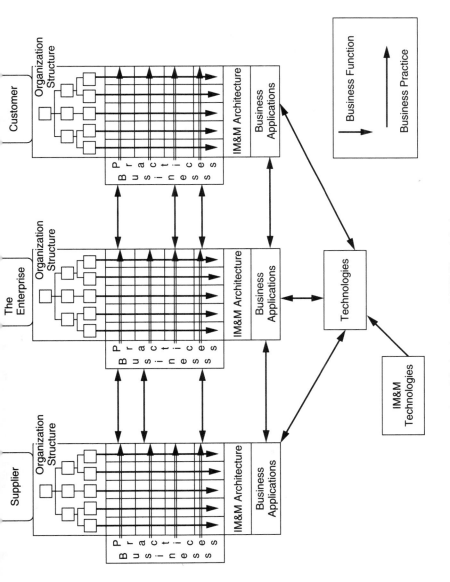

Figure 5.1 Management perspective of the business and IM&M revisited.

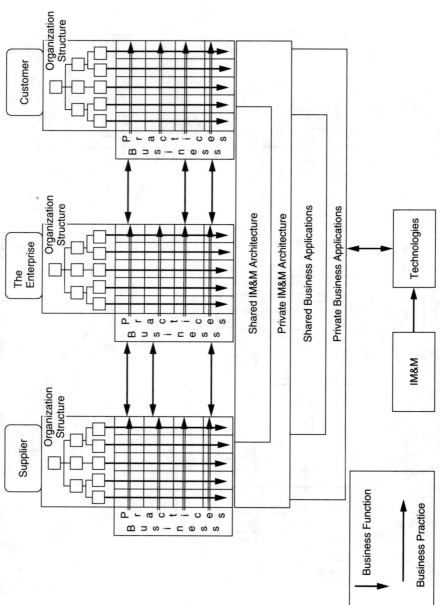

Figure 5.2 Customer, supplier, and the enterprise as one.

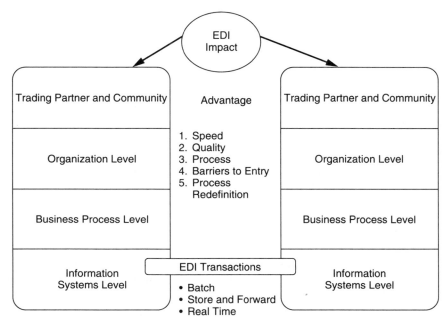

Figure 5.3   Electronic commerce.

■ *Commentary:*   This is an interesting issue because it implies that IM&M has intrinsic value. If you recall, in Chap. 2, Sec. 2.2, "The Management Perspective," we asserted that IM&M has value only when enabling a business practice. It would therefore seem evident that it is possible to measure information system value only when the business practice advantage accrued.

An excellent example of this is the common concern with the proliferation of LANs across the organization. A typical reaction is, "We can't afford a LAN administrator for every *n* LANs. It's too expensive." Now, let us suppose that the installation and operation of 100 LANs would improve sales by *x* percent, improving net revenue by $30 million. Assuming 50 LAN administrators would cost $5 million, why couldn't you afford them? Why wouldn't you?

The point is repeated: the value of information systems is measurable only in the context of the applications served and enabled. You can't determine any value asynchronously.

Issue 19: Managing dispersed systems

■ *Definition:*   This issue is concerned with how traditional information-systems services can support the larger amount of processing power dispersed across the enterprise. It recognizes that a huge redistribution of the computing power wealth has occurred, and it is concerned

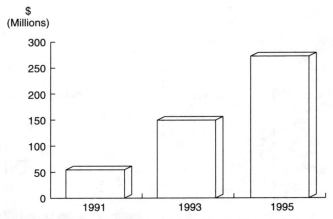

Figure 5.4   Wireless LAN connections forecast. (*Source: IDC*)

with the proper management of the investment. Some consultancies estimate that 70–80 percent of the total corporate MIPS are now located outside the data center.

Issue 20: Capitalize on advances in information technology

- *Definition:*   This issue is concerned with identifying and incorporating new advantageous technology into the enterprise, and is

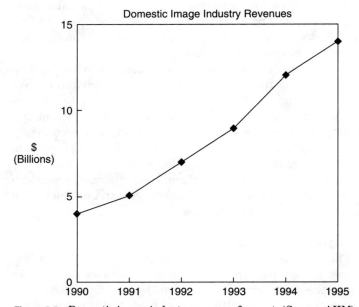

Figure 5.5   Domestic image industry revenue forecast. (*Source: AIIM*)

TABLE 5.1   Pen-based Computing Forecast
Pen-based Computing Will Grow Significantly over the Next Few Years

		Projected Shipments (Units in Thousands)		
1991	1992	1993	1994	1995
30	110	250	500	850

SOURCE: IDC.

closely related to providing new technologies with which to reengineer the business.

- *Commentary:* Three examples can vividly demonstrate the emergence of new technologies that can be incorporated into the technology portfolio for advantage.

1. *Wireless LAN connections* (see Fig. 5.4).   Provides an untethered way to tie mobile employees into LANs and reduce life-cycle LAN maintenance and configuration costs.

2. *Imaging* (see Fig. 5.5).   Provides the framework for reengineering any paper/form-intensive application.

3. *Pen-based computing* (see Table 5.1).   Provides the basis for reengineering any application that traditionally has used clipboardlike devices. Typical applications include field workforce automation, inventory control, insurance adjustment, and quality

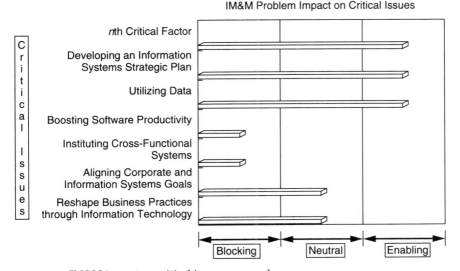

Figure 5.6   IM&M impact on critical issues—example.

TABLE 5.2   Critical Issues Summary

These Are the Critical Success Factors for IM&M Management in the Early 1990s

Issue number	Issue
1	Reshape business practices through information technology
2	Aligning corporate and information systems goals
3	Instituting cross-functional systems
4	Boosting software productivity
5	Utilizing data
6	Developing an information-systems strategic plan
7	Improving software development quality
8	Creating an information architecture
9	Integrating information systems
10	Improving leadership skills in information systems
11	Cutting information systems costs
12	Using information systems for competitive breakthrough
13	Improving the informations systems human resource
14	Educating management on information systems
15	Connecting to customers and suppliers
16	Managing changes caused by information technology
17	Promoting the information system function
18	Determining the value of information systems
19	Managing dispersed systems
20	Capitalize on advances in information technology

control. This technology is moving so rapidly that, since its introduction in August 1991, two variations have been developed: pentop computers (which can also serve as laptop computers) and notebook versions that are two-sided notebook computers.

This chapter has reviewed 20 critical information-systems issues as identified by information-system executives. We will use this knowledge in the next chapter as a way to measure the seriousness of IM&M problems on the enterprise. IM&M pathologies will be viewed as serious when they block the achievement of these objectives. As was the case with the Five Forces factors, we will use an impact graph (as illustrated in Fig. 5.6) to visualize the effect. IM&M problems are viewed as having one of the following types of impact:

- *Blocking.*   The IM&M problem blocks the obtainment of the objective.
- *Neutral.*   The IM&M problem is neutral to the obtainment of the objective.
- *Enabling.*   The IM&M problem enables obtainment of the objective (most unlikely).

Table 5.2 lists the 20 issues in a convenient reference format.

6

The Business Problem

The purpose of this chapter is to analyze the persistent and chronic problems which impede the advantageous use of IM&M in solving business problems. These problems are common throughout the IM&M community and are quickly recognizable in most enterprises. We will accomplish this purpose by analyzing the problem as follows:

- *Section 6.1: The Medical Model.* This section will explain the Medical Model of illness as a way to understand and structure the IM&M illnesses that are infecting the corporate body.

- *Section 6.2: The Pathology of IM&M.* This section will diagnose the problems encountered in IM&M by use of the Medical Model.

- *Section 6.3: Competitive Disadvantage.* This section will qualitatively measure the severity of the inflicted illnesses. It will accomplish this by first analyzing how the IM&M problems deplete the competitive health of the firm (using the Five Forces Model laid out in Chap. 3 as the analytical yardstick), and then by analyzing how the IM&M problems block the realization of the critical information systems issue reviewed in Chap. 5.

- *Section 6.4: Conclusions.* This section will summarize the essential points of the chapter.

The use of the Medical Model as the vehicle to diagnose the problems associated with IM&M is an extremely powerful approach. Not only does it deepen our understanding of the problem and structure the analysis, but (since the problem will be divided into symptoms—pathology and etiology—later when we prescribe client/server computing as a therapy) it will also enable us to understand exactly what component of each IM&M illness we are treating and the prognosis for long-term, interim, or temporary relief.

6.1   The Medical Model

Figure 6.1 illustrates, from a lay perspective, the structured approach medicine takes to understand illness and the different facets of it. The Medical Model divides the problem into three major components: assessment, diagnosis, and treatment. The Medical Model is a complete methodology; it partitions the problem of illness to allow concentration of effort, is holistic, recognizes the limits of therapy, permits multiple treatments, is recursive, and understands the difference between symptoms, pathology, and etiology of illness. Illness (see Fig. 6.1) can be divided into three discrete but interlocking components:

1. *Symptoms.* Symptoms are the external manifestation of illness. These are the visible or testable signs that show something is wrong. Clusters of symptoms that congregate together to suggest a specific disease are called a *syndrome.* Symptoms normally provide the immediate motivation for taking therapeutic action to relieve the discomfort. When the therapy treats only the symptoms, the pathology remains but is temporarily masked.

2. *Pathology (disease).* Pathology is the specific bodily element that is ill. It is the malfunctioning organ (or other bodily part) whose malfunction is causing the symptoms. The pathology expresses itself through symptoms. When therapy treats the pathology, the disease is eliminated—but it can return.

3. *Etiology.* The etiology is the underlying root cause of the illness. It identifies the originating agent that caused the pathology. When you eliminate the etiology of an illness, the root cause is extinguished, so the illness will not return.

This is a very powerful analytical model to use in diagnosing a problem and distinguishing between the superficial problem, the malfunctioning component, and the true root cause of the problem. Later, when one attempts to treat the problem, having analyzed it in this context, it is easier to determine which of the following applies.

- You are providing symptom relief.
- You are healing the diseased function.
- You are eradicating the causative agent.

Medical Model

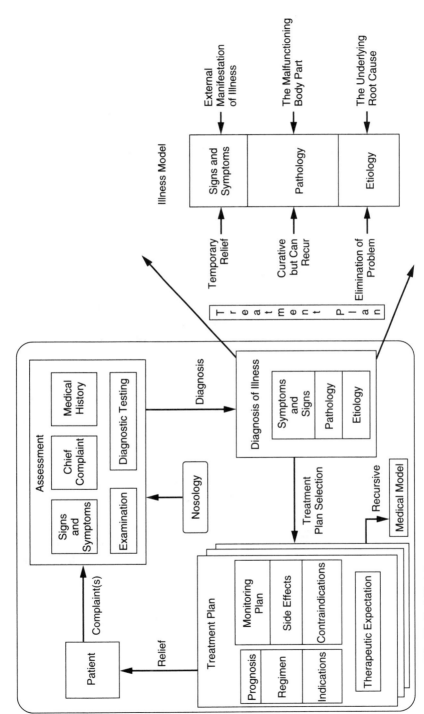

Figure 6.1 The Medical Model.

73

Obviously, the long-term efficacy of the prescribed therapy will be quite different depending on what you are treating. This explains why so many "cures" prescribed by IM&M industry gurus do not have enduring efficacy. When the problem analysis is restricted to "It takes too long, costs too much, and isn't what I wanted anyhow," only symptoms are being identified. The recommended prescriptions only mask the symptoms, offering interim relief but, since neither the pathology nor the etiology have been attacked, the illness reasserts itself after the temporary remission. One needs to understand which component of the diagnosis is being treated by the prescribed therapy.

6.2   The Pathology of IM&M

The purpose of this section is to understand which IM&M illnesses afflict the corporate body. This analysis will be structured after the Medical Model that was explained in the preceding section. Having analyzed IM&M problems with the insight gained from the Medical Model, we will be positioned to later demonstrate the efficacy of client/server computing, not merely in relieving the symptoms of the IM&M problems, but in many cases attacking both the pathology and the etiology.

What are some of these symptoms? From a wide range of sources— vendor literature, industry trade magazines, conference proceedings, books, consultant reports, personal business experience, etc.—it would appear evident that, as currently applied, IM&M demonstrates symptoms such as rigid/inflexible systems, high maintenance costs, a data mess, poor system documentation, user dissatisfaction, dependency on application gurus, fragility of applications (a house of cards), proprietary solutions, tunnel thinking and solutions (one size/solution fits all), resistance to change, monolithic systems, and dependence on obsolete technologies.

While this might not be a complete list nor include all of your favorites, it is representative of the types of persistent problems associated with IM&M, and is quite adequate to allow for a diagnosis.

Table 6.1 analyzes the symptoms relative to the traditional disadvantage criteria of cost, time, and functionality. A "P" indicates the primary disadvantage, and an "S" indicates the secondary disadvantage. Notice that the summation of the disadvantages is "immobility."

If we were constrained by traditional analysis, we would now be done. However, using the Medical Model, we can probe for deeper insight and define five illnesses. The IM&M illnesses will be presented using the structure of *illness, symptoms, pathology,* and *etiology.*

TABLE 6.1   IM&M Symptom Disadvantages

The Symptoms Sum to the Composite Symptom of Immobility

Symptoms	Competitive disadvantages		
	Cost	Timeliness	Functionality
Rigid/inflexible systems		P	S
High maintenance cost	P	S	
Data mess	P	S	
Poor system documentation	P	S	
User dissatisfaction	S		P
Dependency on application gurus	S	P	
Fragility of applications	P	S	
Proprietary solutions	S		P
Tunnel thinking and solutions		S	P
Resistance to change		S	P
Monolithic systems		P	S
Dependency on obsolete technologies	S		P
Immobility	P	P	P

6.2.1   Illness: Processing architecture disability

This may be described as the inability to exploit processing architecture to derive competitive advantage for the firm.

Symptoms:

- Rigid/inflexible systems

- High maintenance costs

- Fragility of systems

- User dissatisfaction

- Monolithic systems

- Reliance on obsolete technologies

Pathology: A kludge of weak architectures applied on an application-by-application basis.

Etiology: An emerging and immature technology discipline.
    This etiology deserves some elaboration, since immaturity sits at the roots of most of the disabilities. Figure 4.14, "Evolution of an Engineering Discipline," introduced in Chap. 4 to explain the preponderance of weak architectures, can again be employed to help explain the problem. Much of what has been done to date in applying IM&M, whether in terms of processing architecture, data architecture, and/or software development, has been characteristic of the craft stage. It should not be surprising, therefore, that when intuition and brute force

sit at the roots of our IM&M solutions (as opposed to formal theories and proven practices), the craft stage in which we have been results in kludges. If you seriously question this analysis, I suggest that you candidly compare the education, professional affiliations, practices, and certification of your system architects, database designers, software developers, and data architects with those of civil engineers, chemical engineers, or mechanical engineers. The difference in the maturity of these disciplines versus IM&M will be evident.

6.2.2   Illness: Software disability

This involves the drag that software development and maintenance place on the ability of the organization to build new advantageous applications.

Symptoms:

- High maintenance costs
- Poor documentation
- User dissatisfaction
- Dependency on gurus
- Resistance to change

Pathology: Use of low-level software tools, lack of process, and resistance to moving software development/maintenance to the "software engineering" stage from the craft stage.

Etiology: Immaturity of discipline, lack of enabling tools, and artisan heritage.

This etiology, as is true with the previous one, is rooted in the youth of software development as an engineering discipline. As a craft, however, software development has built upon the artisan model (i.e., virtuoso work that is highly creative, unique, and nonrepeatable). Artists are to be prized, but great art has some discomforting attributes for a mass industry like software development: it is expensive; it is slow; only a relatively small group of individuals can do it; and it is not subject to a repeatable process. If IM&M is ever to reach its full potential for aiding the organization, software development must be built on an engineering model, not an artisan model.

This view of the state of software development is supported by work done at Carnegie Mellon University. The Systems Engineering Institute at Carnegie Mellon has devised a Process Maturity Framework for

Software Design. This framework defines five levels of software development maturity as follows:

Level 1: Chaotic
- Poor management disciplines
- Ill-defined procedures
- Serious cost and schedule problems
- Ad hoc and inconsistent software life-cycle processes
- Little use of modern software tools and technology

This level is characteristic of 74 to 86 percent of all software development.

Level 2: Repeatable
- Repeatable standard processes are used for cost estimating, scheduling, change management, and reviews throughout the software life cycle.

This level is characteristic of 22 to 23 percent of all software development.

Level 3: Defined
- Complete development process is defined.
- Definition encompasses analysis, design, code, review, and training.

This level is characteristic of 1 to 4 percent of all software development.

Level 4: Managed
- The entire process is quantified, measured, and well-controlled.
- It is tool-based.
- There is continual improvement of the process.

This level is characteristic of 0 percent of all software development.

Level 5: Optimized
- Optimization of Level 4 processes
- Prevention studies
- Cause-effect analysis

This level is characteristic of 0 percent of all software development.

This Carnegie Mellon Process Maturity Framework, when coupled with Fig. 4.14, "Evolution of an Engineering Discipline," would clearly support the assertion that software development is characteristic of the craft stage.

6.2.3   Illness: Data disability

This is the inability to manage and exploit data as a critical corporate asset.

Symptoms:

- High maintenance costs
- Data mess
- User dissatisfaction
- Dependence on obsolete technologies

Pathology: Dedicated file and closed database architectures as the foundation for managing the corporate data resource. (Refer to Chap. 4, Sec. 4.2, "Data Architecture," for a review of these data environments.)

Etiology: An immature discipline that has refused to adapt available data-engineering principles.

While the state of engineering advancement may be arguable for processing architecture and software development, such is not so with data engineering. Of all the IM&M engineering disciplines, data engineering has made the greatest progress by far in achieving the engineering stage, and there exist well-established principles and processes for analyzing, modeling, and administrating data. In most companies, they are simply not implemented.

6.2.4   Illness: Organization disability

This involves the inability of the information technology organization to successfully manage and apply the IM&M resources.

Symptoms:

- User dissatisfaction
- Proprietary solutions
- Tunnel thinking and solutions
- Resistance to change

Pathology: Fortress I/T; arrogant and self-serving.

Etiology: A technology, as opposed to a business focus, and a tactical strategy of expediency.

There are many management theorists who give a wide variety of reasons for the failure of management, particularly information technology management, to succeed. While the ability of IM&M management to succeed (given the craft stage of IM&M) was certainly constrained, it would appear that the problem was more than simply being in the wrong place at the wrong time. Many criticisms by Dr. W. Edwards Deming* of management processes seem to apply here:

- short-term focus
- lack of planning
- expediency
- quick results oriented
- lack of leadership

No matter whether you agree with Dr. Deming's overall critique or not, it is clear that management and management procedures of the engineering disciplines would never permit the production implementation of systems with the lack of quality control that is routinely acceptable in IM&M systems development.

What is particularly interesting about these illnesses is that they generally occur together. Most companies experience all of them, not just one or two. There is a composite illness that is describable as follows:

6.2.5 Illness: IM&M disability

This may be described as the collective negative effect that poor processing architecture, data management, software development, and IM&M management have on applying IM&M for competitive advantage.

Symptoms:
- Immobility (the summation of the other twelve)

Pathology:
- Processing architecture kludge
- Data asset mismanagement
- No software engineering
- Fortress I/T

Etiology:
- Immature discipline
- Lack of tools

---

* *Out of Crisis,* Dr. W. E. Deming, 1982, MIT Press.

- Expediency
- Technology focus

The net effect of this illness is to severely constrain the enterprise's ability to maneuver in response to the competitive environment.

6.2.6   Summary

This section has analyzed the problems associated with IM&M by using the Medical Model as the analytical tool. We have demonstrated that the problems associated with IM&M result in four illnesses (plus a composite of the four) that combine to limit the mobility of the organization to deal with its constantly changing environment. Table 6.2 summarizes the diagnoses that were made in this section. In the next section, we will determine the severity of the infliction.

6.3   Competitive Disadvantage

The purpose of this section is to analyze the degree to which the IM&M illnesses identified in the previous section hurt the enterprise. The approach will be twofold. First, the illnesses will be superimposed on the Five Forces Model to assess the degree to which they retard the ability of the enterprise to act and react competitively. Second, the degree to which the IM&M illnesses block the accomplishment of the critical objectives identified in Chap. 5 will be assessed. Impact graphs will be used to illustrate the qualitative effect of the illnesses on both the Five Forces and the critical issues.

6.3.1   Five Forces analysis

Each of the Five Forces and associated factors will be analyzed for impact. For each factor by force, the following will be presented:

- The factor
- Strong competitive health condition
- Weak competitive health condition
- Primary affecting illness
- Commentary on impact

Commonly, an argument can be made that multiple illnesses affect the factor. It is not, however, analytically helpful to list every illness against every factor. Consequently, we will strive to identify only a primary illness and, when clearly required, a secondary illness. In this analysis, no relative weighting is done to any factors.

TABLE 6.2   IM&M Diagnosis

The Application of IM&M Suffers from Four Illnesses and One Composite Illness

Illness model \ Illness	Diagnosis				
	Processing architecture disability	Software disability	Data disability	Organization disability	IM&M disability
Symptoms	1. Rigid/inflexible systems 2. High maintenance costs 3. Fragility of systems 4. User dissatisfaction 5. Monolithic systems 6. Reliance on obsolete technologies	1. Poor documentation 2. High maintenance costs 3. Dependency on gurus 4. User dissatisfaction 5. Resistance to change	1. Data mess 2. High maintenance costs 3. User dissatisfaction 4. Reliance on obsolete technologies	1. Proprietary solutions 2. Tunnel thinking and solutions 3. Resistance to change 4. User dissatisfaction	1. Immobility
Pathology	Weak architectures	Craft	Dedicated file and closed database architecture	Fortress mentality and arrogant/self-serving	1. Processing architecture kludge 2. Data asset mismanagement 3. No software engineering 4. Fortress I/T
Etiology	1. Immature discipline	1. Immature discipline 2. Artisan heritage	1. Immature discipline 2. Refusal to adapt data engineering practices	1. Technology focus 2. Expediency strategy	1. Immature discipline 2. Lack of tools 3. Expediency 4. Technology focus

Force 1: Supplier Power.   The power of the industry suppliers to control prices, quality, and overall conditions of purchase of goods and services.

- *Factor:* Concentration of suppliers

  Strong competitive health: Many suppliers

  Weak competitive health: Few/monopoly suppliers

  Affecting illness: Organization disability

  Commentary: Organizations are tightly coupled to embedded suppliers due to proprietary solutions, resistance to change, and dependence on obsolete technologies.

- *Factor:* Product differentiation

  Strong competitive health: Commodity product

  Weak competitive health: Proprietary product

  Affecting illness: Organization disability and software disability

  Commentary: Organizations are tightly coupled to embedded suppliers due to proprietary solutions, resistance to change, dependence on obsolete technologies, and dependence on technology frozen gurus.

- *Factor:* Switching costs

  Strong competitive health: Low

  Weak competitive health: High

  Affecting illness: Processing architecture disability

  Commentary: Organizations are tightly coupled to embedded suppliers, and gradual migration is difficult due to proprietary solutions, monolithic systems, fragile systems, and dependence on obsolete technologies.

- *Factor:* Substitute products

  Strong competitive health: Many

  Weak competitive health: Few

  Affecting illness: Processing architecture disability

  Commentary: Organizations are tightly coupled to embedded suppliers due to proprietary solutions, resistance to change, and dependence on obsolete technologies.

- *Factor:* Supplier bypass

  Strong competitive health: Not possible

  Weak competitive health: Easily done

  Affecting illness: Not applicable

  Commentary: Why would they want to?

- *Factor:* Importance of customer to supplier

  Strong competitive health: Very important

  Weak competitive health: Unimportant

  Affecting illness: Processing architecture disability

  Commentary: The vendor's knowledge that the customer would incur high switching costs and the absence of substitute products puts the customer at a distinct bargaining disadvantage.

Supplier Power summary. Of the six factors that compose the Supplier Power Force, five are negatively impacted. Figure 6.2 illustrates the negative impact. Table 6.3 shows the specific impact of the disabilities on supplier factors. The IM&M illnesses clearly retard the ability of the enterprise to achieve competitive advantage vis-à-vis suppliers.

Force 2: Buyer Power. The degree to which the buyer's ability to influence price, quality, and the other terms of purchase gives the buyer an advantageous bargaining position.

- *Factor:* Buyer concentration

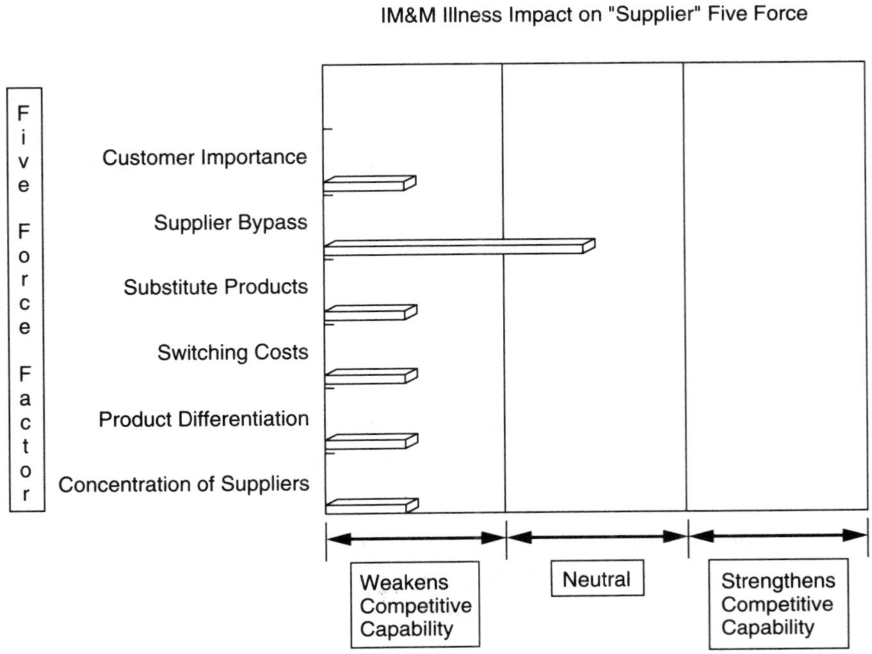

IM&M Illness Impact on "Supplier" Five Force

Figure 6.2   IM&M illness impact on Supplier Power.

TABLE 6.3   IM&M Illness Impact on Supplier Power

Five of the Six Supplier Factors Are Adversely Impacted by the IM&M Illnesses

Force	Factor	IM&M illness			
		Processing architecture disability	Software disability	Data disability	Organization disability
Supplier Power	Concentration of suppliers				X
	Product differentiation		X		X
	Switching costs	X			
	Substitute products	X			
	Supplier bypass				
	Customer importance	X			

Strong competitive health: Diversified group of buyers

Weak competitive health: One buyer

Affecting illness: All

Commentary: The combined illnesses constrain the ability of the organization to offer novel/innovative products/services to attract an ever-expanding customer base.

- *Factor:* Product is commodity

   Strong competitive health: Differentiated product

   Weak competitive health: Commodity product

   Affecting illness: Processing architecture disability and data disability

   Commentary: The data mess, high maintenance costs, monolithic systems, tunnel solutions, and fragility of systems conspire to prevent novel ways to add value to products.

- *Factor:* Product as component of buyer's cost structure

   Strong competitive health: Low percent of cost

   Weak competitive health: High percent of cost

   Affecting illness: All

   Commentary: The combined illnesses conspire to raise the cost of products and services, which is passed on to customers.

- *Factor:* Buyer profitability

   Strong competitive health: Highly profitable

   Weak competitive health: Marginally profitable

   Affecting illness: Processing architecture disability, data disability, and software disability

   Commentary: Improved IM&M could translate into improved products and services that would improve the buyer's value chain, resulting in improved profitability for buyer.

- *Factor:* Product's importance to customer

  Strong competitive health: Critical to customer's product

  Weak competitive health: Required in customer's product

  Affecting illness: Processing architecture disability, software disability, and data disability

  Commentary: Innovative use of IM&M, which could uncover ways to improve value of product to customer and change his or her perspective to product, has immense importance.

- *Factor:* Product viewed as an expense

  Strong competitive health: Product saves customer money or adds differentiated value

  Weak competitive health: Product is pure expense

  Affecting illness: Processing architecture disability

  Commentary: Monolithic and inflexible systems limit options to improve value of product to customer.

- *Factor:* Supplier bypass

  Strong competitive health: Buyer cannot bypass

  Weak competitive health: Buyer can bypass

  Affecting illness: Processing architecture disability, software disability, and data disability

  Commentary: Software disability prevents customizing value-added solutions for customers. Processing architecture disability prevents reacting to customer needs. Data disability prevents knowing the customer.

Buyer Power summary. Of the seven factors that compose the Buyer Power Force, all are negatively impacted. Figure 6.3 illustrates the negative impact. Table 6.4 shows the specific impact of the disabilities on buyer factors. The IM&M illnesses clearly retard the ability of the enterprise to achieve competitive advantage vis-à-vis buyers.

Force 3: Threat of Entry. The threat that new entrants will join the marketplace and compete for market share.

- *Factor:* Economies of scale

  Strong competitive health: Large volumes required

  Weak competitive health: Small volumes which allow for competitive pricing

  Affecting illness: Not applicable

- *Factor:* Product differentiation

  Strong competitive health: Differentiated product

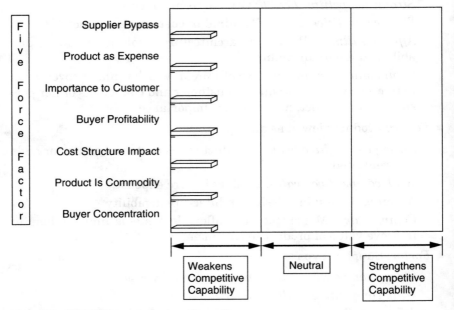

Figure 6.3   IM&M illness impact on Buyer Power.

Weak competitive health: Commodity product
Affecting illness: All
Commentary: All the disabilities converge to inhibit creating products with high barriers to entry.

TABLE 6.4   IM&M Illness Impact on Buyer Power

All the Buyer Power Factors Are Adversely Impacted by the IM&M Illnesses

		IM&M illness			
Force	Factor	Processing architecture disability	Software disability	Data disability	Organization disability
Buyer	Buyer concentration	X	X	X	X
Power	Product is commodity	X		X	
	Product as component of buyer's cost-structure	X	X	X	X
	Buyer profitability	X	X	X	
	Product's importance to buyer	X	X	X	
	Product viewed as an expense	X			
	Supplier bypass	X	X	X	

- *Factor:* Customer switching costs

  Strong competitive health: High

  Weak competitive health: Low

  Affecting illness: All

  Commentary: All the illnesses contribute to inhibiting ability to create products with nuances that add differentiated value to the customer's use of product.

- *Factor:* Capital requirements

  Strong competitive health: High

  Weak competitive health: Low

  Affecting illness: Not applicable

- *Factor:* Non-economy-of-scale advantages

  Strong competitive health: Many

  Weak competitive health: Few

  Affecting illness: Data disability

  Commentary: The data mess prevents knowing customers, bargaining with suppliers, and understanding competitors.

- *Factor:* Distribution channel access

  Strong competitive health: Blocked

  Weak competitive health: Open

  Affecting illness: Processing architecture disability

  Commentary: Horizontal integration with distributors can increase the ante for entry into the market.

- *Factor:* Government policy

  Strong competitive health: Block new entrants

  Weak competitive health: Underwrites new entrants

  Affecting illness: Not applicable

- *Factor:* Retaliation of incumbents

  Strong competitive health: Strong retaliation record

  Weak competitive health: No retaliation history

  Affecting illness: All

  Commentary: All the disabilities limit the ability to react in a manner most advantageous to the situation.

Threat of Entry summary. Of the eight factors that compose the Threat of Entry Force, five are negatively impacted. Figure 6.4 illustrates the negative impact. Table 6.5 shows the specific impact of the disabilities on Threat of Entry factors. The IM&M illnesses clearly retard the abil-

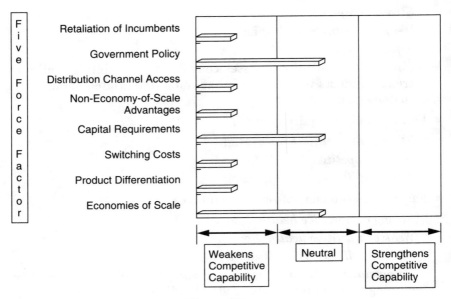

Figure 6.4   IM&M illness impact on Threat of Entry.

ity of the enterprise to achieve competitive advantage vis-à-vis creating strong barriers to market entry.

Force 4: Substitute Products.   The existence of substitute products that constrain the ability of the enterprise to control pricing, quality, and other factors of sale, since there is a point at which the customer will switch.

TABLE 6.5   **IM&M Illness Impact on Threat of Entry**

Five of the Eight Threat of Entry Factors Are Adversely Impacted by the IM&M Illnesses

| Force | Factor | IM&M illness | | | |
		Processing architecture disability	Software disability	Data disability	Organization disability
Threat of Entry	Economies of scale				
	Product differentiation	X	X	X	X
	Customer switching costs	X	X	X	X
	Capital requirements				
	Non-economy-of-scale advantages			X	
	Distribution channel access	X			
	Government policy				
	Retaliation of incumbents	X	X	X	X

■ *Factor:* Strong substitute

Strong competitive health: No
Weak competitive health: Yes
Affecting illness: All
Commentary: All the illnesses conspire to limit the ability to create a product that is difficult to mimic.

■ *Factor:* Substitute price/performance trends

Strong competitive health: Lower than product
Weak competitive health: Better than product
Affecting illness: All
Commentary: All the disabilities limit the ability to accomplish massive productivity improvements (business reengineering) that would translate into price advantage.

■ *Factor:* Profitability of substitute product industry

Strong competitive health: Low
Weak competitive health: High
Affecting illness: Not applicable

■ *Factor:* Competitive rivalry of substitute product industry

Strong competitive health: Low
Weak competitive health: High
Affecting illness: Not applicable

Substitute Product summary.   Of the four factors that compose the Substitute Product Force, two are negatively impacted. Figure 6.5 illustrates the negative impact. Table 6.6 shows the specific impact of the disabilities on Substitute Product factors. The IM&M illnesses retard the ability of the enterprise to achieve competitive advantage vis-à-vis combating substitute products.

Force 5: Rivalry of Existing Competitors.   The degree to which existing competitors battle for market share.

■ *Factor:* Number and equality of competitors

Strong competitive health: Few and smaller
Weak competitive health: Many and larger
Affecting illness: All
Commentary: All the illnesses conspire to limit the ability to maneuver.

■ *Factor:* Market growth

Strong competitive health: High

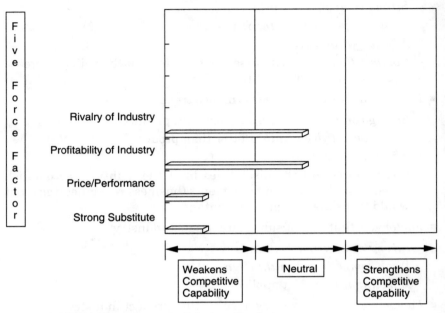

Figure 6.5   IM&M illness impact on Substitute Products.

Weak competitive health: Negative
Affecting illness: Data disability
Commentary: Poor data analysis limits the ability to analyze market segments and/or discover new market segment opportunities.

- *Factor:* Product differentiation

  Strong competitive health: Differentiated

TABLE 6.6   IM&M Illness Impact On Substitute Products

Half the Substitute Product Factors Are Negatively Impacted by the IM&M Illnesses

		IM&M illness			
Force	Factor	Processing architecture disability	Software disability	Data disability	Organization disability
Substitute Products	Strong substitute	X	X	X	X
	Substitute price/ performance	X	X	X	X
	Profitability of Substitute Product industry Competitive rivalry of Substitute Product industry				

Weak competitive health: Commodity

Affecting illness: All

Commentary: All the illnesses conspire to limit the ability to create a product that is difficult to mimic and creates unique value for the customer.

- *Factor:* Customer switching costs

    Strong competitive health: High

    Weak competitive health: Low

    Affecting illness: All

    Commentary: All the illnesses conspire to limit the ability to create a product that is difficult to mimic and creates unique value for the customer.

- *Factor:* Fixed costs

    Strong competitive health: Low

    Weak competitive health: High

    Affecting illness: All

    Commentary: All the illnesses conspire to limit the ability to create innovative ways to reengineer business processes to lower fixed costs.

- *Factor:* Unit of capacity increment

    Strong competitive health: Low

    Weak competitive health: High

    Affecting illness: Not applicable

- *Factor:* Exit barriers

    Strong competitive health: Few

    Weak competitive health: Many

    Affecting illness: Not applicable

- *Factor:* Diversity of corporate personalities

    Strong competitive health: Same

    Weak competitive health: Different

    Affecting illness: Data disability

    Commentary: Lack of good data management limits competitive intelligence.

Rivalry of Existing Competitors summary. Of the eight factors that compose the Rivalry Force, six are negatively impacted. Figure 6.6 illustrates the negative impact. Table 6.7 shows the specific impact of the disabilities on Rivalry factors. The IM&M illnesses clearly retard the ability of the enterprise to achieve competitive advantage vis-à-vis combating existing rivals.

IM&M Illness Impact on "Rivalry of Existing Competitors" Five Force

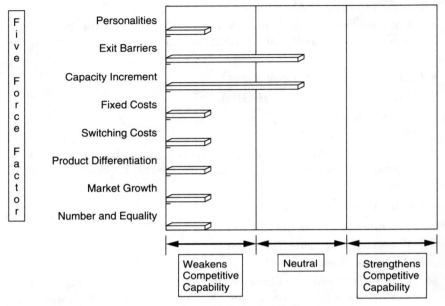

Figure 6.6 IM&M illness impact on Rivalry of Existing Competitors.

TABLE 6.7   IM&M Illness Impact on Rivalry of Existing Competitors

Six of Eight Rivalry Factors Are Adversely Impacted by the IM&M Illnesses

		IM&M illness			
Force	Factor	Processing architecture disability	Software disability	Data disability	Organization disability
Rivalry of Existing Competitors	Number and equality of competitors	X	X	X	X
	Market growth			X	
	Product differentiation	X	X	X	X
	Customer switching costs	X	X	X	X
	Fixed costs	X	X	X	X
	Unit of capacity increment				
	Exit barriers				
	Diversity of corporate personalities			X	

Five Forces analysis summary. This section has analyzed the impact that the IM&M illnesses have on the competitive health of the enterprise. The following conclusions are warranted:

1. The competitive health of the enterprise is severely compromised by the current state of IM&M.
2. All the IM&M illnesses have a significant negative impact.
3. Processing architecture disability and data disability have the largest impacts, with software disability occurring slightly less often.
4. Strategic action is required by IM&M management to remedy this serious situation.

6.3.2   Critical issues analysis

The purpose of this section is to assess the degree to which the IM&M illnesses erect barriers to achieving the critical issues objectives. This barrier analysis complements the previous Five Forces analysis as a way to judge the severity of the IM&M illnesses. Obviously, the more barriers they present to achieving these vital objectives, the more severe the illness. For each critical issue, the following structure will be used:

- The issue
- The primary affecting illness which raises a barrier
- Commentary on impact

As was the case with the preceding analysis, we will attempt to identify only a primary illness per issue. No relative weighting of the critical issues is considered in this analysis, although the issues are presented in the priority order provided from the Index Group research. The impact of the IM&M illnesses on the critical issues of information systems management are as follows:

- *Issue 1:* Reshaping business practices through information technology
  Barrier: All
  Commentary: This is a massive undertaking requiring the maximum contribution from all facets of information technology to succeed.
- *Issue 2:* Aligning corporate and information systems goals
  Barrier: Organization disability
  Commentary: This is clearly a management issue of becoming customer-focused, aligning technology with business needs, and taking a long-term (as opposed to an expedient) strategy in delivering solutions.

- *Issue 3:* Instituting cross-functional systems

  Barrier: Data disability and processing architecture disability

  Commentary: Accomplishment of this objective mandates the creation of shared data resources and a processing architecture infrastructure to permit access and interoperability.

- *Issue 4:* Boosting software development productivity

  Barrier: Software disability

- *Issue 5:* Utilizing data

  Barrier: Data disability

  Commentary: While data disability is clearly the primary barrier, the framework of a processing architecture that permits distributed access from heterogeneous information appliances is a close second.

- *Issue 6:* Developing an information system strategic plan

  Barrier: Organizational disability

  Commentary: This is a management issue which has to include strategies for dealing with the data mess, the processing architecture mess, and the software development mess.

- *Issue 7:* Improving software development quality

  Barrier: Processing architecture disability and software disability

  Commentary: The inclusion of software disability as a primary barrier is obvious. Processing architecture is included because of its inheritable character. If we view quality as providing solutions that meet customer needs, the ability of the software to leverage the foundation architecture is critical to accomplishing quality.

- *Issue 8:* Creating an information architecture

  Barrier: All

  Commentary: This is a vital undertaking requiring the maximum contribution from all facets of information technology to achieve.

- *Issue 9:* Integrating information systems

  Barrier: Processing architecture disability

  Commentary: Interoperability is a processing architecture issue.

- *Issue 10:* Improving leadership skills in information systems

  Barrier: Not applicable

- *Issue 11:* Cutting information system costs

  Barrier: All

  Commentary: A discontinuous improvement of radical dimension requires attacking this problem on all fronts. The synergy resulting from the alignment of all the areas (processing, data, organization, and software) in a healthy state would significantly attack this problem.

- *Issue 12:* Using information systems for competitive breakthrough

  Barrier: All

  Commentary: This is a vital undertaking requiring the maximum contribution from all facets of information technology to achieve.

- *Issue 13:* Improving the information system human resource

  Barrier: Organizational disability

  Commentary: This is a management issue that will require revision of the human resource systems to influence/promote positive behaviors. (This will be discussed in Chap. 8, "Implementing Client/Server Computing.")

- *Issue 14:* Educating management on information systems

  Barrier: Not applicable

  Commentary: The best education would be by demonstration of aligning information systems with business capability requirements.

- *Issue 15:* Connecting to customers and suppliers

  Barrier: Processing architecture disability and data disability

  Commentary: The most atomic point of interface is a datum. Given that data definitions are agreed upon, it is necessary to interoperate without the requirement that everybody use one vendor's proprietary solution. This requires a powerful processing architecture—an architecture with reach.

- *Issue 16:* Managing changes caused by information technology

  Barrier: Not applicable

- *Issue 17:* Promoting the information system function

  Barrier: All

  Commentary: It will be difficult to promote the function and prove the IM&M asset value unless all the illnesses are alleviated. The situation is insidious. As some are cleared up, the others will just take on a more glaring presence. All the illnesses have to be eradicated.

- *Issue 18:* Determining the value of information systems

  Barrier: Not applicable

- *Issue 19:* Managing dispersed systems

  Barrier: All

  Commentary: To preempt entropy, this will require a complete information architecture be put in place.

- *Issue 20:* Capitalizing on advances in information technology

  Barrier: Processing architecture

  Commentary: This requires an infrastructure that permits the easy addition of new components.

Critical issues analysis summary.   This section has analyzed the barriers that the IM&M illnesses have erected to block achievement of the critical issue objectives. Figures 6.7, 6.8, and 6.9 depict the barrier impact graphically. Table 6.8 illustrates the specific barrier(s) erected against each critical issue. The following conclusions are warranted:

1. The ability to achieve the critical issue objectives is severely blocked.

2. All the IM&M illnesses have a significant blocking effect.

3. Processing architecture disability is the most recurring illness (though all the illnesses occur almost half the time).

4. Remedial action will be required by strategic IM&M management to alleviate the blocked condition.

6.4   Conclusions

This chapter has analyzed the problems associated with IM&M by use of the Medical Model analytical method to diagnose the types of ill-

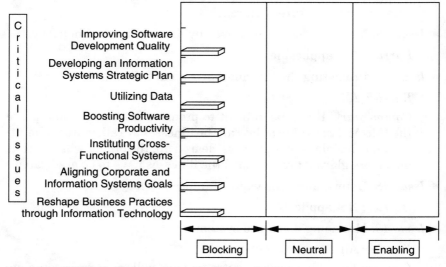

Figure 6.7   IM&M illness impact on critical issues I.

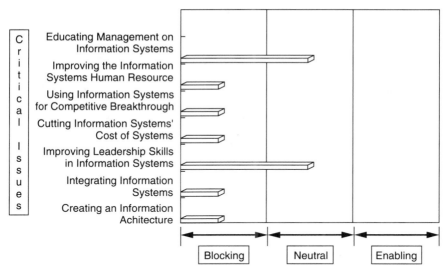

Figure 6.8   IM&M illness impact on critical issues II.

nesses affecting the corporate body. We used the Five Forces Model and critical issues list to determine the severity of the inflictions. The following conclusions are warranted:

1. IM&M is suffering from four discrete but interrelated illnesses:
   - Processing architecture disability

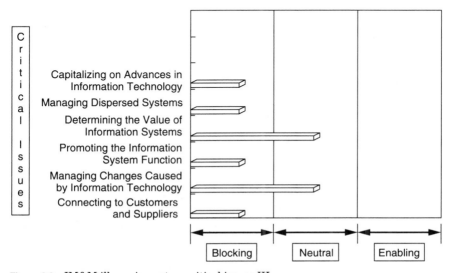

Figure 6.9   IM&M illness impact on critical issues III.

TABLE 6.8   IM&M Illness Impact on Critical Issues

Remedial Action Will Be Required to Alleviate the Blocked Condition

Critical issues	IM&M illness			
	Processing architecture disability	Software disability	Data disability	Organization disability
Reshape business practices through information technology	X	X	X	X
Aligning corporate and information systems goals	X			
Instituting cross-functional systems	X		X	
Boosting software productivity	X			
Utilizing data	X			
Developing an information systems strategic plan	X			
Improving software development quality	X		X	
Creating an information architecture	X	X	X	X
Integrating information systems	X			
Improving leadership skills in information systems				
Cutting information systems costs	X	X	X	X
Using information systems for competitive breakthrough	X	X	X	X
Improving the informations systems human resource	X			
Educating management on information systems				
Connecting to customers and suppliers	X	X		
Managing changes caused by information technology				
Promoting the information system function	X	X	X	X
Determining the value of infor- mation systems				
Managing dispersed systems	X	X	X	X
Capitalize on advances in information technology	X			

- Data disability
- Software disability
- Organizational disability

2. The four illnesses most often occur together and can be referred to collectively as *IM&M disability:* the total negative effect that the underlying disabilities have on the competitive health of the enterprise. The overriding symptom of this condition is *immobility:* the inability of the enterprise to maneuver in response to the competitive environment. The illnesses constrain both the needed reach and range of the IM&M resource (see Fig. 3.5, "Reach and Range").

3. The Five Forces analysis indicates that the impact of the illnesses is severe; the IM&M illness constrains the ability of the enterprise to compete and develop competitive advantages.

4. The critical issues analysis confirms the Five Forces analysis in that the impact is blocking the achievement of critical information technology objectives.

5. A strategic response is required by IM&M management to alleviate this serious challenge to the continued well-being of the enterprise.

The required strategic response is the repositioning of the IM&M architecture from $P_{\text{host-centered computing}}$ to $P_{\text{client/server computing}}$, which will be explained in the next two chapters.

7

Client/Server Computing

The purpose of this chapter is to develop a complete understanding of what client/server computing is, its advantages and, specifically, how it provides therapy for the various IM&M illnesses that were documented in the previous chapter. As is characteristic of emerging technologies, there is a wide range of opinion on the value of client/server computing. At one extreme, reminiscent of the PC fanatics of the early 1980s, there are true zealots who believe client/server computing is the ultimate technology. Just as every application then could be solved with a PC and a spreadsheet, every application now can be solved with a workstation, LAN, and set of servers. At the other extreme, there are the persistent pessimists who believe nothing will ever change (i.e., host-centered mainframe computing "now and forever"). Their world is comfortably immutable. At the center sit the pragmatists who do not view technology either obsessively or defensively, but seek continued new advantage in change and adaptation. We mediate this spectrum of opinion and demonstrate the significant new advantages that client/server computing does offer as follows:

- *Section 7.1: Definition.* This section will provide a robust definition of client/server computing.

- *Section 7.2: Why Now.* This section will answer the common question of the zealot, pessimist, and pragmatist: Why now? What convergence of events/forces has conspired to make client/server computing viable in the early 1990s? If it is so great, why didn't we do it before?

- *Section 7.3: Database Servers.* This section will analyze the characteristics of database server technology. The positioning of databases as shared data repositories is the premier application of client/server computing and requires explicit focus to understand its advantages.

- *Section 7.4: Competitive Advantage.* This section will redo the analysis done in Chap. 6, "The Business Problem," but now demonstrates how client/server computing alleviates the IM&M illnesses that were diagnosed. Each illness will be reviewed for client/server therapeutic affect. The Five Forces Model will be reanalyzed to understand how client/server computing improves competitive position, and "The Critical Issues" (see Table 5.2) will be reanalyzed to decide how client/server computing enables the critical information systems objectives to be achieved.

- *Section 7.5: Conclusions.* This section will summarize the major conclusions of this chapter.

Chapter 8, "Implementing Client/Server Computing," will complete the analysis of client/server computing by explaining the issues surrounding a successful implementation.

7.1   Definition

Client / server computing is a processing architecture in which a single application is partitioned among multiple processors which cooperate in a unified manner to complete the unit of work as a single task. The more rigorous definition used throughout this book is as follows:

> Client/server computing is a processing model in which a single application is partitioned among multiple processors (front-end and back-end), and the processors cooperate (transparent to the end user) to complete the processing as a single, unified task. A client/server bond product ties the processors together to provide a single-system image (illusion). Shareable resources are positioned as servers offering one or more services. Applications (requestors) are positioned as clients which access authorized services. The entire architecture is endlessly recursive; in turn, servers can become clients and request services of other servers on the network, and so on and so on.

Figure 7.1 illustrates the client/server concept and depicts many key attributes of the client/server environment as follows:

- Multiple clients may access multiple servers.
- Multiple servers may be accessed by multiple clients.
- A server may provide multiple services.
- A service may be offered by multiple servers.
- The architecture is endlessly recursive; servers may, in turn, act as clients and request services from other servers.
- Because of the preceding attributes, the architecture is understood to be a "many-to-many" architecture. This clearly distinguishes it from the "one-to-many" architecture attribute of the traditional host-

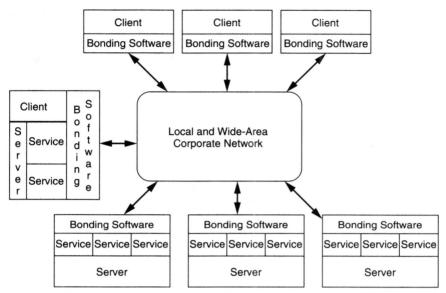

Figure 7.1   Client/server computing: many clients/many servers.

centered computing environment (see Fig. 1.2, "Host-Centered Computing Architecture").

- Local and wide area networking are used to tie the geographically dispersed clients and servers together.

- A software layer called *bonding* software is resident on both clients and servers, and handles the message routing between participants. The bonding software is the facility that provides the illusion of a single system to the user. Bonding software is also commonly referred to as *middleware*.

In the industry literature, client/server computing is referred to by all of the following names:

- Client/server architecture
- Client/server computing architecture
- Requester/server architecture
- Workstation/server architecture
- Network computing
- User-centered computing
- Desktop-centered computing.

Despite the label given and the different accent put on client/server computing as a consequence, they all refer to the model of computing illustrated in Fig. 7.1.

Some analysts view client/server computing as the fourth wave of computing (see Fig. 7.2). Economic theory postulates that technology progresses through major technology transformations, i.e., Kondratiev Waves. Client/server computing is the fourth subwave of the "Electronics and Information Technology" Kondratiev Wave. The client/server subwave consolidates the advantages of the previous computing subwaves by permitting all the previous computing models to interoperate.

In client/server computing, the work is split between cooperating processors. Figure 7.3 illustrates how clients and servers may have the basic services of presentation, processing, and data partitioned across participating processors. The client may utilize shared resources from multiple servers to complete a unit of work. Servers may be general-purpose computers, specialized computers optimized for a specific task, or multitasking workstations/PCs. Although database access stands out as the most advantageous and obvious shared service (Sec. 7.3, Database Servers, will expand on this point), any activity that can be positioned as a general utility or reusable service (communication, numeric-intensive computing, electronic mail/fax, graphics, peripheral sharing, etc.) or could benefit from dedicated and/or specialized hardware/software is a server candidate. An enterprisewide connectivity architecture consisting of local area networking, metropolitan area networking, and wide area networking interconnects the clients to the servers. Figure 7.4 illustrates these ideas. Applications on appropriately scaled and functional clients perform part of the business function. Reusable and shareable resources required by the application are provided by an appropriate server. Servers, when required, take on the role of client to each other in order to avail themselves of each other's services.

Client/server computing is built upon a cooperative processing, or peer-to-peer, architecture (see Fig. 4.11, "Cooperative Processing Architecture"). A cooperative processing architecture uses a peer-to-peer communications protocol (such as LU 6.2 or TCP-IP) to allow two programs to have an interactive conversation. In this model, each program executes an interactive verb set to carry on the conversation. Each participant in the interactive dialogue has to anticipate and handle all possible requests and replies. This includes error recovery. The client/server bonding software places a layer of software above the peer-to-peer protocol that vastly simplifies the application programming and hides the underlying protocol from both the clients and the servers. The application accesses the bonding software through an application program interface (API). An API is provided on each side of the conversation, and it is through the hiding provided by the API that the illusion of a single system is created for both the clients and servers. The most common bonding software APIs are Remote Procedure Calls (RPCs) and Structured Query Language (SQL). Figure 7.5 illustrates the RPC

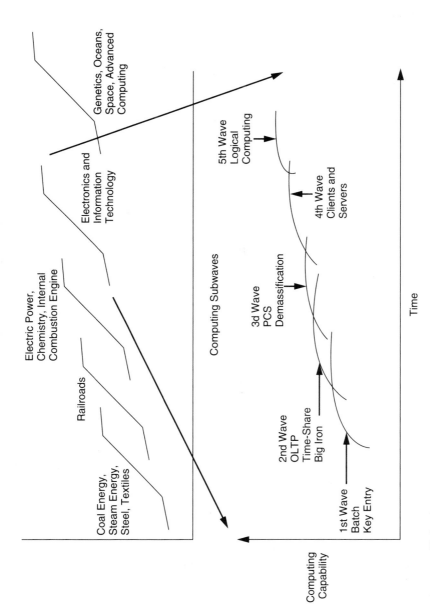

Figure 7.2 Technology waves.

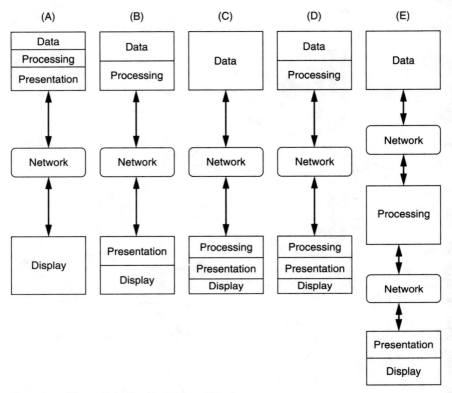

Figure 7.3 Alternative client/server partitioning.

idea. It is transparent to both the requestor and the server that the interaction is occurring over a network and, in fact, the transparency hides the physical location of both.

Figure 7.6 illustrates a typical data access request within the SQL client/server environment as follows:

1. Sitting at a personal computer, a user performs data entry using a graphical user interface (GUI).

2. As required, the application processing layer issues SQL requests for data that is passed through the bonding software transparently over the network to the server.

3. The server performs the request.

4. Rows, flags, errors, and status are returned.

5. The answer is displayed back to the user at the client personal computer.

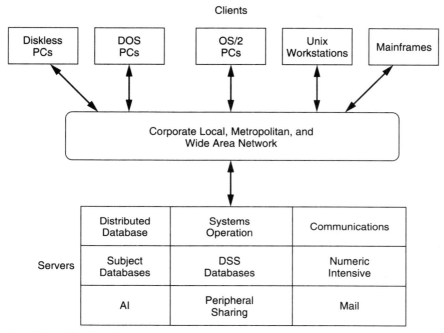

Figure 7.4 Clients and servers.

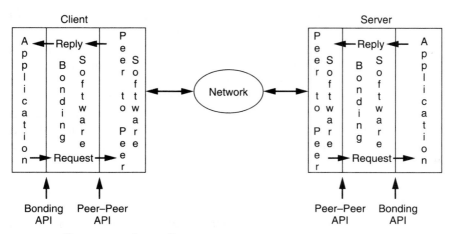

Figure 7.5 Remote procedure call.

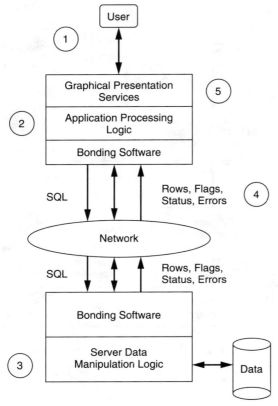

Figure 7.6   SQL: client/server interaction.

Client/server computing, consequently, provides a vehicle to bond together the dispersed islands of processing that exist within the enterprise. It provides an architecture that allows a *network* of computers (rather than individual computers) to solve a problem. It does not always eliminate and replace the other architecture models, but it does provide a powerful architectural solution for those users demanding to share resources and dispersed computing power in synchronization with favorably changing computing economics. Figure 7.7 illustrates in more detail how the information processing architecture of the 1990s will evolve into networks of networks of computing.

7.2   Why Now?

The purpose of this section is to provide an understanding of the events that have occurred that make client/server computing not only desirable from a business perspective, but practical from a technology per-

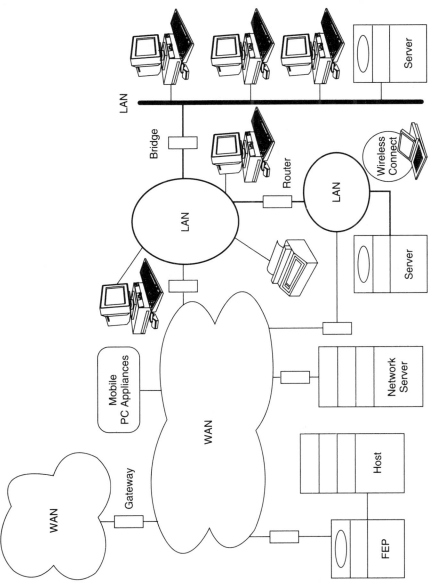

Figure 7.7 IM&M architecture of the 1990s.

spective. It answers the common question of both the zealot and the cynic: Why now? What has occurred that makes client/server computing doable in the early 1990s?

The answer to this question is rooted in the convergence of six factors that are illustrated in Fig. 7.8.

1. *Enduring need.*   Business has a relentless requirement for new competitive advantages. It is constantly seeking solutions to better protect itself against the Five Forces that were discussed in Chap. 3.

2. *IM&M illness.*   The current deployment of IM&M has resulted in the illnesses discussed in Chap. 6. Competitive advantage-hungry businesses are looking for novel solutions.

3. *Changing computing economics.*   The changing economics of computing have made *downsizing* (the movement of all or part of an application to microprocessor-based computing platforms) extremely attractive.

4. *Division of labor.*   Accompanying the downsizing of computing has been the emergence of feature/functionality that was not possible in the traditional host-centered processing environment. Nevertheless, the traditional host-centered environment has retained capa-

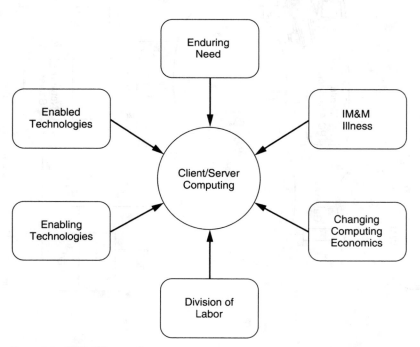

Figure 7.8   CSC: Why now?

bilities that are not easily migrated to the downsized environment. The result is the requirement to partition applications and place feature/functionality where most advantageous.

5. *Enabling technologies.* A necessary set of prerequisite technologies have come into place to enable bonding to take place.

6. *Enabled technologies.* Client/server computing facilitates the deployment of other technologies that are advantageous but best deployed within the client/server framework. Client/server computing is a necessary stepping-stone to these desirable solutions.

The answer to the "Why now?" question is the fortunate convergence of all these factors to create the necessary environment. Each factor will now be discussed in more detail.

Enduring need: competitive advantage.   This issue was fully discussed in Chap. 3. The requirement for competitive advantage is the enduring need for business survival. IM&M solutions that enable the enterprise to adapt and to maneuver are in constant demand.

IM&M illnesses.   This issue was fully developed in Chap. 6. IM&M is viewed as pathological—inflicting the business with immobility rather than the necessary maneuverability. The enduring need for competitive advantage from IM&M, coupled with the IM&M illness, creates a fertile ground for substitute solutions to grow.

Changing computing economics.   A substitute product becomes extremely attractive when it demonstrates superior price/performance trends (part of the Five Forces Model). This is exactly what has been occurring with regard to microprocessor-based computing relative to minicomputer or mainframe computing. Figures 7.9 to 7.14 illustrate this situation from several perspectives.

Figure 7.9 shows both the economic and raw performance advantages of VLSI, RISC, and symmetric multiprocessing solutions over traditional processing technology.

Figure 7.10 shows the accelerating price/performance advantage that PC (CISC and RISC) technologies enjoy over other technologies.

Microprocessor performance is measured by the three dimensions of clock speed, transistor density, and instructions per cycle. Figure 7.11 shows the improvement in clock speeds for each x86 microprocessor.

Figure 7.12 complements the previous illustration and shows the anticipated performance trends for the other two dimensions of microprocessor performance, transistor density, and instructions per cycle. Representatives of Intel, in press interviews, have discussed a project called *Micro 2000.* Micro 2000 would have the following attributes:

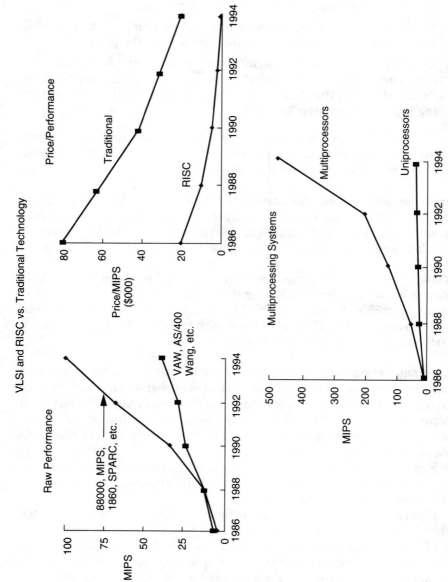

Figure 7.9 VLSI and RISC vs. traditional technology. (*Source: The Gartner Group*)

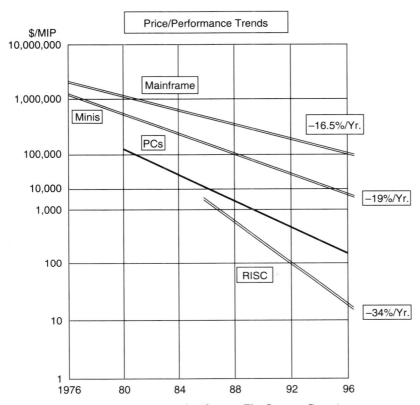

Figure 7.10 Price/performance trends. (*Source: The Gartner Group*)

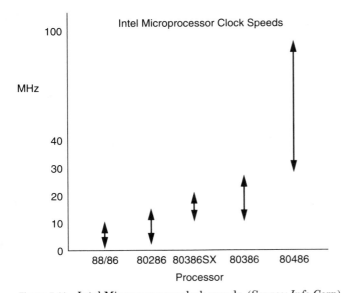

Figure 7.11 Intel Microprocessor clock speeds. (*Source: Info Corp*)

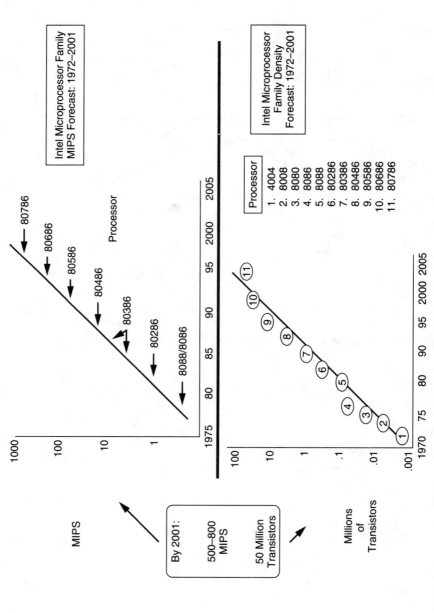

Figure 7.12 Intel Microprocessor family MIPS and density forecast. (*Source: Info Corp*)

1. 50–100 million transistors with each transistor ⅟₂₅ the current size
2. 250-MHz clock speed
3. multiprocessing CPU with four processors rated at 700 MIPS/CPU
4. 2-megabyte cache memory
5. x386 compatibility
6. graphics unit with HDTV quality full-motion video
7. applications in telepresence, speech recognition, handwriting recognition, virtual reality, and artificial intelligence

Figure 7.13 highlights the incredible price/performance gap accelerating between mainframes and micro-based systems.

Figure 7.14 shows the ever-increasing amount of desktop MIPS that will be purchasable for a constant $5000.

The simple, obvious, and irrefutable conclusion from this sample of evidence is that micro-based computing provides an extraordinarily

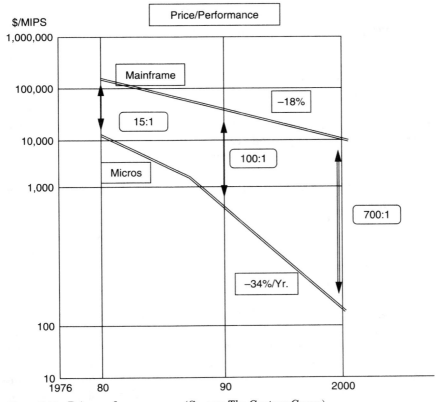

Figure 7.13   Price performance gap. (*Source: The Gartner Group*)

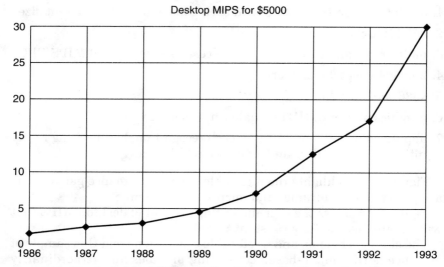

Figure 7.14   Rise in desktop MIPS per dollar. (*Source: The Gartner Group*)

attractive price/performance substitute to traditional mainframe computing.

One may argue that while they are inexpensive, they are not well used. On a utilization basis, traditional mainframe MIPS are much more cost effective. While this is indeed true today, this argument emphasizes the point—it does not counter it. With all those inexpensive MIPS deployed and underutilized, there is a huge underutilized asset waiting to be exploited. Client/server computing provides the architecture to improve the utilization of all those dispersed micro-based MIPS.

Complementing the astounding price/performance economics of microprocessors is the related improvement in price performance and density of memory chips, as illustrated in the following figures.

Figure 7.15 shows the history and forecast of memory-chip density.

Figure 7.16 demonstrates the impressive price/performance trends for chip memory.

Recent industry announcements demonstrate a similar cost situation with regard to DASD storage systems. A 20-gigabyte storage system on a LAN server sells for ⅟₃₄ the cost per byte of mainframe storage, and ⅕ the cost per byte of minicomputer storage. Figure 7.17 illustrates the anticipated cost declines in PC storage systems. These memory and storage trends simply serve to make the previously demonstrated microprocessor economics even more irrefutable. The economics of computing have clearly shifted in favor of micro-based processors at the expense of the traditional mainframe solution.

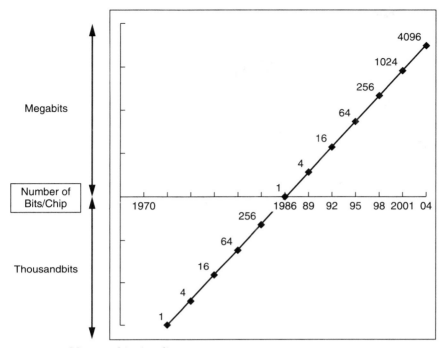

Figure 7.15 Memory chip time-line.

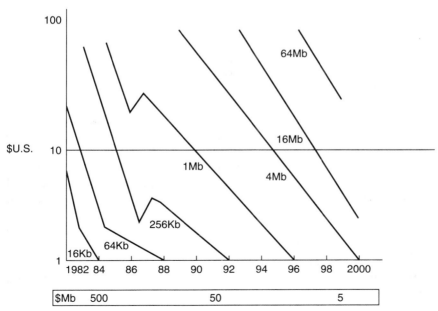

Figure 7.16 Dynamic Random Access Memory (DRAM) pricing history and forecast. (*Source: Info Corp*)

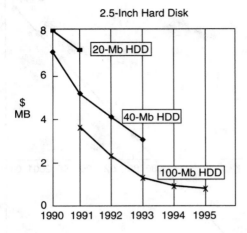

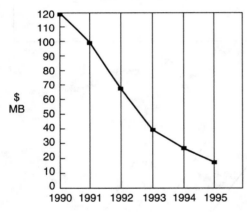

Figure 7.17   Declining cost of flash and hard-disk memory. (*Source: Input*)

Division of labor.   The Five Forces Model demonstrates that a substitute product is attractive when it experiences superior price/performance trends, and when it is a strong substitute. A product is a strong substitute when it demonstrates equal and/or superior functionality to the reference product. Microprocessor-based systems can and do provide novel functionality. Features which are obtainable on a PC or workstation, graphical user interface, multimedia support (voice, video, image), WYSIWYG word processing, etc. are simply not obtainable within the host-centered architecture.

Concurrently, many services traditionally provided by the host-centered architecture, such as the following, are not readily dispersed to client sites.

- corporate data management
- 24/7 operation

- batch processing management
- security
- archival management
- foreign media management

Consequently, the need arises for a division of labor with feature/ functionality being dispersed to where it optimizes the work flow. Client/server computing provides the necessary architecture to synthesize the advantages of each platform.

Enabling technologies. This term refers to various technological developments whose advent was a prerequisite to enable client/server computing to become operational. The key enabling technologies that have emerged are as follows:

Open systems. Open systems provide a set of standards across heterogeneous supplied platforms that enable portability, scalability, interoperability, data access, and appliance connectivity. They create the necessary standards to allow a bonded world. The astronomical permutations involved in connecting all proprietary solutions to all proprietary solutions would have made bonding impractical. The clear convergence of the industry to open systems with a few proprietary solutions (such as IBM SAA and DEC AIA) provides an environment in which interoperability can occur.

Standards are generally provided by five classes of entities:

1. Public groups such as ANSI, IEEE, CCITT, and ISO
2. Industry groups such as X/OPEN, UI, OSF, COS, UNIFORUM, and SQL-ACCESS
3. Users such as the United States military, FIPS, and influential buyers such as GM with MAP and Boeing with TOP
4. Consortiums such as the X-Window consortium
5. Suppliers such as IBM (SAA), Microsoft (DOS), and AT&T (NFS)

Supplier standards represent de facto standards by virtue of market presence, and are the least open.

Standards of particular concern to the client/server computing environment are itemized in Table 7.1. Users should participate and track the development of standards, since greater adherence to standards is critical to enable the previously mentioned advantages of scalability, portability, interoperability, data access, and appliance connectivity.

The standards' movement has strategic importance far in excess of just enabling client/server computing. The imposition of standards into the computing industry fundamentally changes the industry structure

TABLE 7.1   Open Standards

Standards Are Vitally Important to Client/Server Computing

Standards body	Standard	Client/server importance
X-Windows consortium	X.11.3	Enables networking of graphical user interface between heterogeneous processors
ANSI	C programming language: ANSI X.3JIIC	Enables portability and scalability
	COBOL programming language: ANSI X.323	Enables portability
	SQL data definition, manipulation and administration language: ANSI X3.135 levels 1 and 2	Enables portability and interoperability
	Electronic data interchange (EDI) ANSI X.12	Enables interoperability
	Remote data access	Enables interoperability
Military	TCP-IP Standard: 1777-78	Enables interoperability
IEEE	POSIX operating system interface: P1003.n	Enables portability, scalability, and interoperability
ISO	OSI 7-layer standards	Enables interoperability

from supplier power to buyer power. Using the Five Forces Model again, as illustrated in Figs. 7.18 through 7.22, critical competition factors such as switching costs, barriers-to-entry product differentiation, concentration of suppliers, and strong substitutes are all redefined in favor of the customer.

Structured Query Language (SQL). SQL is a nonprocedural data definition, manipulation, and administration language. Unlike previous generation data languages, it is completely independent of the physical structure of the database, so it is immune to the physical structure of the database and the geographical dispersion of the data. SQL provides the necessary bonding API to allow remote data access.

Graphical user interfaces (GUI). Graphical user interfaces such as Windows, Open Look, X-Windows, etc. create a far superior user interface compared to traditional full-screen and character interfaces that are characteristic of the host-centered computing environment. Such interfaces require processing capability at the user terminal. The desire to improve user ergonomics through such superior interfaces provides an incentive for distributed processing and the need to permit the GUI user access to nonimmediate services.

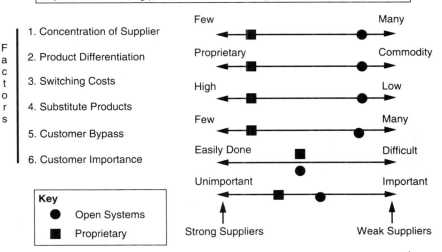

Figure 7.18   Open systems and Supplier Five Force.

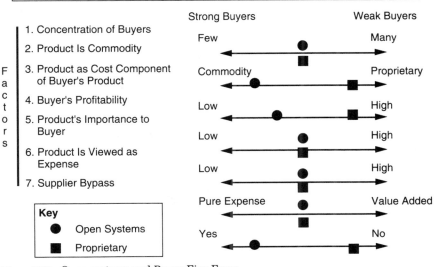

Figure 7.19   Open systems and Buyer Five Force.

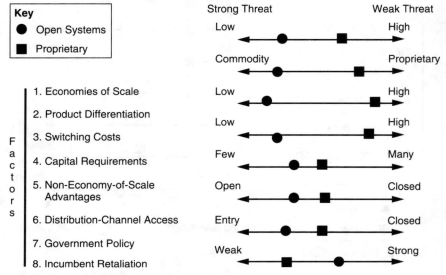

Figure 7.20 Open systems and Threat of Entry Five Force.

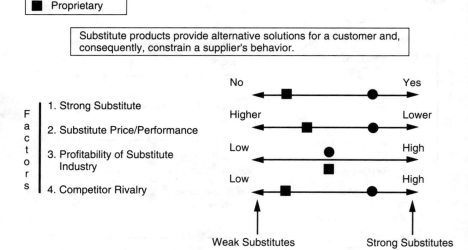

Figure 7.21 Open systems and Substitute Product Five Force.

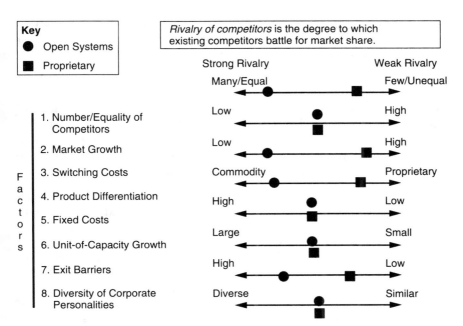

Figure 7.22   Open systems and Rivalry Five Force.

Cooperative processing protocols.   Cooperative processing communication protocols provide the necessary peer-to-peer capability to permit bonding software to build upon. Wide adoption of protocols such as LU 6.2, TCP-IP, and OSI provide the necessary low-level communication interface for friendlier bonding products to be constructed.

Bonding software/middleware.   Bonding software provides the required APIs which applications write to. Bonding software simplifies the entire client/server environment for the user as it hides all the underlying complexities of networking. Examples of bonding software are TUXEDO/T, Oracle SQL-Net, and Sybase Open Server.

Server machines.   Server machines provide the inevitable specialization of function that one would anticipate within a client/server environment. Vendors optimize servers for specific functions and, in doing so, offer superior price/performance and/or enriched functionality. Two excellent examples of server machines are the Teradata DBC for data management and the KORBX processor for linear programming problems.

Networking bandwidth.   Interoperability through networking (local, metropolitan, and/or wide area) is a basic attribute of client/server computing. Figure 7.23 illustrates the history and future of networking bandwidth. Gigabyte and terabyte bandwidths that will be provided through optical fiber will be required to handle the tremendous communications traffic of a bonded world. Figure 7.24 shows the growth of communication bridges and routers that are used to interconnect LANS. The increased bandwidths will be required to support the ever-growing inter-LAN traffic.

Enabled technologies.   Enabled technologies are the complement of enabling technologies. They represent desired solutions that are best delivered within a client/server framework because of administration, cost, shareability, security, etc. Client/server computing becomes the enabler for the following desired technologies.

Multimedia.   Imaging, voice, video, and graphics require the existence of distributed intelligence (and in large doses). Multimedia will have a tremendous impact on business reengineering. With work-flow management software, it will provide a new approach to managing the avalanche of paper with which business must contend each year. Some analysts forecast that while U.S. business currently handles over 380 billion documents a year, that number will rise to 800 billion by 1995. Reengineering will be required to handle such a deluge of form processing. Some obvious applications for multimedia are:

- Financial document management

- Customer service

- Employee records management

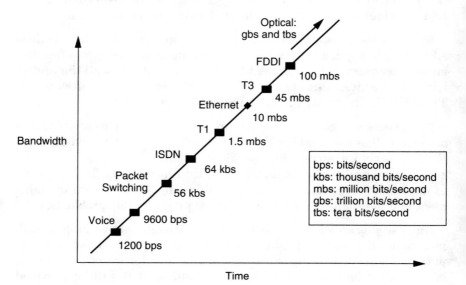

Figure 7.23   Networking bandwidth.

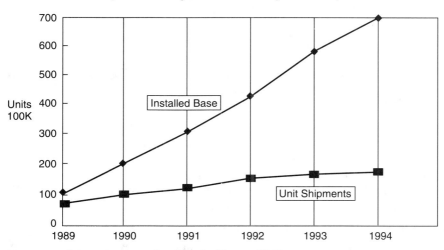

Figure 7.24   Internetwork market growth. (*Source: IDC*)

- Medial records
- Security identification

The client/server architecture provides the optimum architecture for these multimedia solutions.

Distributed database.   Distributed database is the technology that permits multiple discrete and dispersed physical databases to be viewed and treated logically as a single unified database. A user could access data from multiple databases without having to deal with the underlying physical dispersion. Distributed database is a critical technology to enable the sharing of data, and it is built on a client/server foundation. Section 7.3 will discuss DDBMS in detail.

Specialized servers.   The ability to decouple processing will spur the development of a side range of specialized servers that perform specific functions in a superior price/performance manner. Monolithic systems could not take advantage of discrete specialization. Client/server computing enables entrepreneurs to develop advantageous and specialized solutions with the ability to plug them into the network due to modularity and interoperability.

Specialized client appliances.   Given the ability to bond, other entrepreneurial vendors will develop optimized information collection, presentation, and preparation appliances to match the exact requirements of different business practices. Solutions will be available specific to the needs of the business practice.

Artificial intelligence. Artificial intelligence will be enhanced by client/server computing in two ways.

- As a processing-intensive application, specialized servers may be deployed as needed.

- Linkage will be made between the AI shells and SQL to allow the AI products to become expert aids for users sitting at their multimedia workstations.

Computer Aided Software Engineering (CASE). CASE is an emerging technology that provides a mechanized development environment for software developers. Developers have requirements for both powerful individual work spaces and sharing. Client/server computing provides an excellent framework to deliver CASE tools that enable both individual and group software development productivity.

Work-flow management software. Work-flow management software permits the scheduling and routing of documents between a work group. The concept serves to improve productivity by permitting concurrent processing of documents and assuring proper routing and completion of work steps. This type of product is designed for a workstation/server user environment.

Summary. This section has answered the valid question of "Why now?" The answer is convergence—the convergence of six factors that make client/server computing both desirable and possible. Figure 7.25 illus-

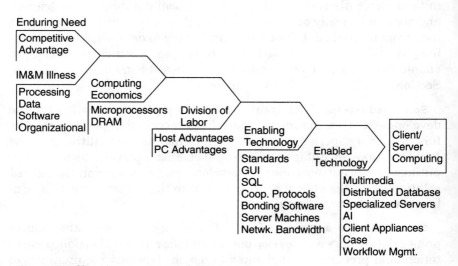

Figure 7.25 Client/server cause-and-effect graph.

trates the merging of causes to enable client/server computing. The enduring need for competitive advantage, coupled with the failures of IM&M, created a fertile environment for the emergence of substitute products. The astonishing price/performance trends of microprocessing, coupled with novel feature/functionality, makes microprocessor-based solutions extremely attractive—especially when division of labor allows placing function where it is most advantageous. It should be clear from this analysis that what we don't have here is a fad; rather, we are living through a fundamental change in computing. In the next chapter, we will call this a *paradigm shift*—a fundamental shift in which the locus of computing moves to the desktop from the host computer. (See Fig. 7.26.) Fads are solutions for transient and shallow needs. Client/server computing, on the other hand, meets the most fundamental business need: the need for competitive advantage.

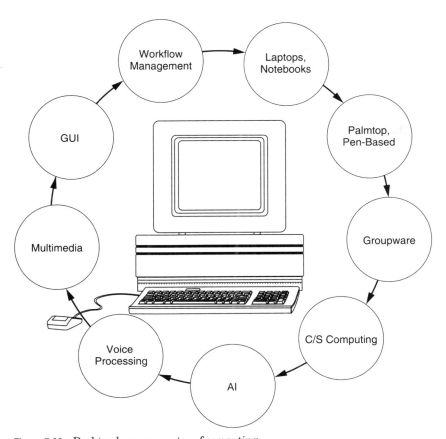

Figure 7.26   Desktop becomes center of computing.

7.3   Database Servers

The purpose of this section is to focus on the especially important subject of database servers. Clearly, the most strategic and premier application of client/server technology is the corporatewide sharing and accessibility of data. As was discussed in Chap. 2, Sec. 4.2, Data Architecture, the dual database architecture:

1. maximizes data quality

2. maximizes data accessibility

3. maximizes data sharing

4. eliminates unplanned-for redundancy

5. simplifies interapplication interaction

6. assures data standardization

7. maximizes application life-cycle productivity

8. accelerates the development of new applications that can reuse the in-place data resource

9. enables the creation of centers of excellence in data management to protect the data asset

The decoupling of data from specific applications and positioning it as an authorized service is a critical step to accomplishing the goal of treating data as a corporate asset. As illustrated in Fig. 7.27, data, not hardware or software, is the critical asset of the enterprise in the 1990s.

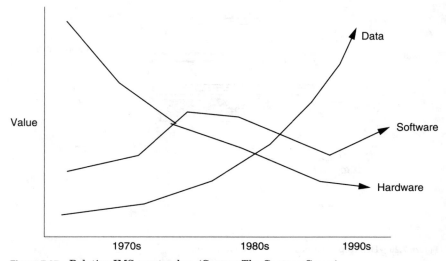

Figure 7.27   Relative IMS asset value. (*Source: The Gartner Group*)

The remainder of this section will review database servers from two perspectives:

1. *Traditional database issues.* This subsection will review the baseline issues commonly involved in selecting databases in the host-centered architecture environment.

2. *Database server issues.* This subsection will analyze major issues in product selection because of positioning the DBMS as a server.

The analysis will focus on issues of relevance for strategic decision making and will, again, not delve into the detailed technical issues.

7.3.1 Traditional DBMS issues

Database is a core IM&M technology and is arguably the most important. Criteria for evaluation and selection are well known and documented, and the DBMS subindustry is extremely innovative and competitive. Baseline criteria for the selection of a DBMS product are generally as follows:

1. *Performance.* The ability of the DBMS, on a given hardware/operating system platform, to handle a specified workload. Performance is routinely measured by transactions per second (TPS) or 95 percent response level (i.e., the response time in which 95 percent of all transactions completed). More sophisticated performance approaches also include time measurements for activities such as:

   - database loading
   - backup
   - restore
   - database restructuring

2. *Data model.* The data model (hierarchical, network, inverted, relational, and/or object) that the DBMS supports and the degree of conformance to the asserted model.

3. *Sizing.* The total amount of data (application data plus access overhead storage [pointers, indexes, etc.]) that the DBMS can manage. This would include space-planning flexibility (i.e., the options for distributing the database across channels, DASD, and explicit placement of records).

4. *The vendor.* An assessment of the overall suitability of the vendor as a supplier of a critical technology. Subissues would include education, support, references, financial situation, user groups, and methods of product quality control.

5. *Data definition and manipulation languages.* The alternative languages made available to the various users (database administrator, developer, and end user) to define, administer, and access the database.

6. *Database administration tools.* An assessment of the depth and breadth of DBMS administration tools available from database conception to retirement. Typical tools would include:

- design aids
- space-planning aids
- database sizing aids
- database restructuring tools
- index checker/repair tools
- pointer checker/repair tools
- log analyzers
- journal management tools
- performance analyzer tools

7. *Operations support.* An assessment of the features which make the product "production able." Typical features would include:

- startup/shutdown procedures
- journal/log management
- automatic restart
- production master administration capability

8. *DBMS internals.* An assessment of the internal DBMS design issues that are critical to DBMS integrity. Typical issues include:

- atomicity
- locking
- memory management
- space management
- single/multithreading
- recoverability

These are all traditional baseline issues of evaluation and are not abrogated by the movement to DBMS servers. DBMS servers require these features plus additional ones, due to the migration of the DBMS to the role of DBMS server in the client/server environment.

7.3.2 DBMS server issues

In migrating to a DBMS server environment, there are seven issues of strategic concern as follows:

1. *Performance optimization.*   How does the server maximize perfor-mance in the client/server environment?

2. *Portability/scalability.*   Can the server be moved between processors?

3. *Standards adherence.*   Does the product adhere to relevant stan-dards for networking, DBMS (SQL), security, etc.?

4. *The vendor as quality partner.*   Can you work with the vendor on a long-term basis to cooperatively improve the quality and adaptabil-ity of the product to your environment?

5. *Operational features.*   Is the product production administrable in the client/server environment?

6. *Server positioning.*   Which DBMS servers will be positioned on which platforms for which applications?

7. *Distributed DBMS.*   Can the product now or in the future support distributed DBMS technology?

Each of these topics will now be discussed separately.

Performance optimization.   The client/server architecture is character-ized, by definition, as requiring extensive interactive data movement between cooperating processors over local and/or wide area networks. Figure 7.28 illustrates the flow of a database transaction in the host-centered computing environment. In this model, all the application pro-gram data manipulation is done, at worst, at channel/disk access speeds and, at best, at memory speeds (data is already in memory cache buffers). If you compare this with Fig. 7.6, it is obvious that there is a potential performance bottleneck due to the frequency of data manipulation requests over the network and the associated speed of the network.

It is, consequently, advantageous to select products that provide capability to control the volume of messages required to complete a transaction. One would want a DBMS server that has included some subset of the following features that can be used, as required, to mini-mize network traffic:

1. *Dynamic SQL caching.*   This feature enables the DBMS to remem-ber the access plan for a repeated set of SQL statements that are dynamically interpreted.

2. *Precompiled SQL.*   This feature results in the database access plan being resolved at compilation and eliminates the need for access plan development at execution.

3. *SQL macros.*   This features permits a group of SQL statements to be packaged as a named macro that can be invoked by the macro name with substitution for specified arguments.

4. *Event-driven triggers.* This feature permits the programmer to explicitly associate programs with database manipulation (add, modify, retrieve, delete) events. The associated program is automatically invoked whenever the data manipulation verb is executed.

5. *Referential integrity.* This feature enables the declaration of integrity rules between entities (i.e., to add entity *a,* entity *b* must be present). As is true with SQL macros and event-driven triggers, this feature reduces the number of requests that have to cross the network to complete a transaction.

6. *Data compression.* This feature enables the product to use a data compression algorithm to reduce the volume of data which crosses the network. It trades processor time (compressing and decompressing) for network transmission time.

The basic principle is simple: for a given network request, one would like to get as much data manipulation performed as possible.

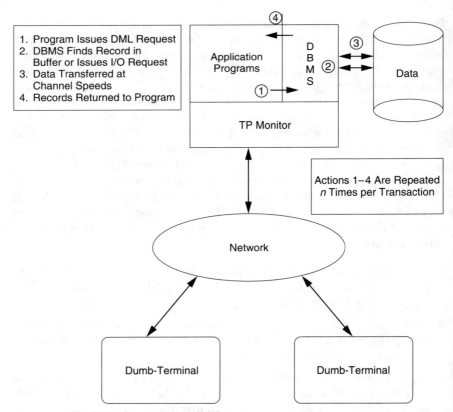

1. Program Issues DML Request
2. DBMS Finds Record in
   Buffer or Issues I/O Request
3. Data Transferred at
   Channel Speeds
4. Records Returned to Program

Application Programs

DBMS

Data

TP Monitor

Actions 1–4 Are Repeated
n Times per Transaction

Network

Dumb-Terminal

Dumb-Terminal

Figure 7.28 Traditional transaction model.

Portability/scalability.   The client/server architecture is advantageous because it enables maneuverability. Toward that end, we would desire the following feature/functionality of the product:

1. *Portability.*   The DBMS product should be available on the set of hardware/OS platforms that we wish to interconnect now and into the future.

2. *Scalability.*   The DBMS product should not only be literally portable, but it should take advantage of the underlying capabilities of the platform. For example, if the ported platform is a multiprocessor environment we would want the DBMS server to multitask in order to take advantage of the parallel processing. Conversely, we would like it to be multithreaded in a uniprocessor environment.

3. *Synchronization.*   The vendor must be able to synchronize the availability of a common release of the product on the targeted set of platforms. This is required to enable cross-platform development and minimize release confusion/chaos and the associated support headaches.

4. *Concurrent execution.*   Multiple releases of the product must be able to execute concurrently and independently on a given platform. This is required to enable gradual and orderly migrations.

5. *Backward compatibility.*   New releases of the product must be able to run prior release programs without change. It will be impossible to flash-cut all users on a network to a new release at once. Migration must permit intermixing releases.

Standards adherence.   The DBMS should adhere to the relevant networking and SQL standards at the API level.

The vendor as quality partner.   The quality of the vendor takes on even greater significance than in the host-centered world. In designing, building, and operating client/server solutions, the IM&M organization must reposition itself as a systems integrator. (See Chap. 8, "Implementing Client/Server Computing.") The ability to integrate is bounded by the quality of the received components. Consequently, it is critical that you select a vendor that you can work with on a long-term basis in order to continually improve quality and coordinate releases.

Operational features.   In a client/server environment, operational issues take on a higher dimension of complexity than in the host-centered world. Clients can fail, the network can fail, or the server can fail. Clients and/or servers have to be dynamically varied on- or off-line. Software has to be distributed throughout the network and installed in a coordinated manner. All this requires a new generation of operations support software.

Server positioning.   In moving to a client/server-based architecture as illustrated in Fig. 4.15, "Optimum IM&M Architecture," it is beneficial to clarify the positioning of DBMS servers by platform, application type, and size. This clarifies the "fog of technology" and makes the DBMS choices explicit. Table 7.2 presents a structured way to organize the database server portfolio. Three discrete roles are identified as follows:

1. *Corporate server (CS).*   The DBMS is used to manage corporate data. The environment is transaction-intensive with an emphasis on sharing data, performance, data accessibility, integrity, recoverability, and availability. The database stores the official corporate "data of record." Corporate servers provide data management for OLTP and OSS applications.

2. *Application server (AS).*   The DBMS is used to manage data for an application and is the shared focal point of a family of applications. The environment is transaction-intensive, with similar concerns to the CS environment. Application servers are also used to manage data in a light record-keeping office environment. Application servers provide the data manager for OLTP, OSS, and time-share applications.

3. *Decision-support server (DS).*   The database is used to support decision-support, information retrieval, what-if analysis, ad hoc reporting, and/or generic information retrieval/analysis applications. The environment is light interactive update- and high query/retrieval-intensive. Decision support servers provide the data manager for information center applications.

Distributed DBMS.   By far, the most strategic add-on feature for DBMS servers is the emerging ability to support distributed DBMS technol-

TABLE 7.2   DBMS Role Matrix

DBMS Products Should Be Positioned by Platform and Role

			Platform 1	Platform 2	Platform 3	Platform n
R	CS	High volume				
o	AS	High volume				
		Low volume				
l		Office				
e	DS	High volume				
		Low volume				
		Personal				

ogy (see Fig. 7.29). A distributed DBMS permits multiple physical discrete DBMS (local and/or remote) to be logically viewed as a single DBMS. Distributed DBMS have the following major requirements:

1. *Location transparency.* The requestor sees a single logical view of the multiple physical databases with no knowledge of the location or partitioning of the underlying databases. Physical databases can be relocated and restructured without the knowledge of the requestor as long as the logical view is still createable.

2. *Performance optimization.* The Distributed DBMS optimizer makes all accessing navigation decisions without input from the requestor. Navigation decisions consider processor capabilities, line speeds, and data distribution.

3. *Copy transparency.* The Distributed DBMS is able to automatically perform both deferred and real-time copy management.

4. *Transaction transparency.* The Distributed DBMS is able to perform atomic transactions (i.e., updating across multiple physical databases while insuring integrity). This capability is referred to as a *two-phase commit*—all the databases commit or none of the databases commit.

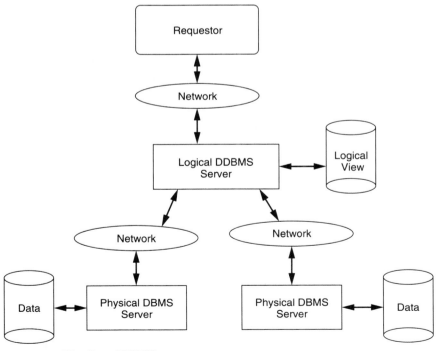

Figure 7.29   Distributed DBMS.

5. *Fragmentation and partitioning transparency.* Database table can be partitioned and/or fragmented across the physical databases but treated as one logical database.

6. *Schema change transparency.* The schema definition of the DBMS can be changed at the appropriate node and the changes rippled and coordinated with other impacted catalogs across the DDBMS system.

7. *Local DBMS transparency.* The DDBMS is able to do all of the above functions with a heterogeneous set of DBMS products, platforms, and networking.

DDBMS is attempting to create the advantage of enormous flexibility in managing the data resource that is an important contributor to maneuverability. As illustrated in Fig. 7.30, a given database could be divided in any of five ways as follows:

1. *Single copy database.* All data entities and instances exist only within a single database.

2. *Partitioned database.* The entities are stored nonredundantly in multiple physical databases. Partitioning is done by entity types. An entity type exists in one and only one partition. All entity instances are only located in the partition to which the entity type is assigned.

3. *Fragmented database.* The entities are stored nonredundantly in multiple physical databases. The entire database schema (all entity types) is mapped to each database, but entity occurrences are distributed (fragmented to each database based on "key" value). Each fragment database is a complete database for some "key" value sets.

4. *Hybrid database.* The entities are stored nonredundantly in multiple physical databases. The databases are a combination of partitioned and fragmented databases.

5. *Replicated database.* The data entities are shared nonredundantly in a single copy, partitioned, fragmented, or hybrid database and, in addition, a replicated database is maintained in sync or deferred copy mode with the copy of record. The replicated copy may have any of the following characteristics:

   Recursively, it may be a single copy, partitioned, fragmented, or hybrid database.
   It may be organized differently than the primary copy.
   It may be an incomplete view of the data.
   It may be an incomplete value set of the data.

The ability of a Distributed DBMS to permit you to organize the data asset in any of these ways and change the underlying physical distribution as required adds tremendous adaptability to the data asset.

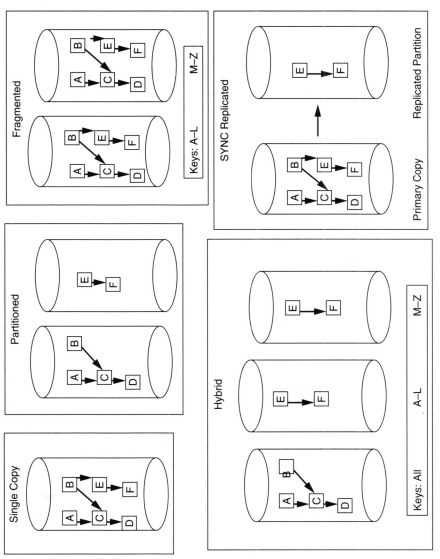

Figure 7.30 Alternative database designs.

137

The following advantages are typically given for DDBMS:

1. It permits you to leverage the downsizing trends.
2. It enables scalability and portability of applications.
3. Copy management enables the dual database architecture.
4. The logical transparency feature permits redeployment of underlying physical databases without disrupting the applications.
5. Data can be placed most advantageously and redistributed most advantageously based on the geography of updaters, the geography of retrievers, the frequency of updates, the frequency of retrievals, and the placement of administration capabilities.

While all these benefits are clearly helpful, they don't explicitly identify the long-term strategic benefit of DDBMS, which is to reunite the corporate data schema (see Fig. 7.31). In a small business, all the entities and entity instances that comprise the composite corporate information model can fit into one database. Applications can consequently share the same data, and decision makers can access the same copy of record or create a complete "as-of" copy.

For large corporations, due to an abundance of factors (limited technology, development expediency, data volume, transaction volume, complexity, application focus, immature data modeling, backup/recovery windows, etc.), the corporate schema (information model) was dispersed across "islands of information." Due to lack of adequate data administration, however, this resulted in incompatible data definitions.

The strategic objective of DDBMS will be to logically reunite the corporate schema. By building corporate and application family servers and superimposing SQL-based DDBMS on top of them, users will be able to have the benefit of a unified view of the multiple physical databases. There is really only one corporate schema; the multiple databases that are dispersed across the enterprise are there because of limitations of technology. By positioning individual databases as servers and then gradually imposing DDBMS on top of them, a logical corporate schema can be unified with tremendous benefits to extending the range (see Fig. 3.5, "Reach and Range") of the IM&M architecture.

7.4 Competitive Advantage

The purpose of this section is to understand the advantages provided by client/server computing. This understanding will be developed by revisiting the analysis that was done in Chap. 6, "The Business Problem," as follows:

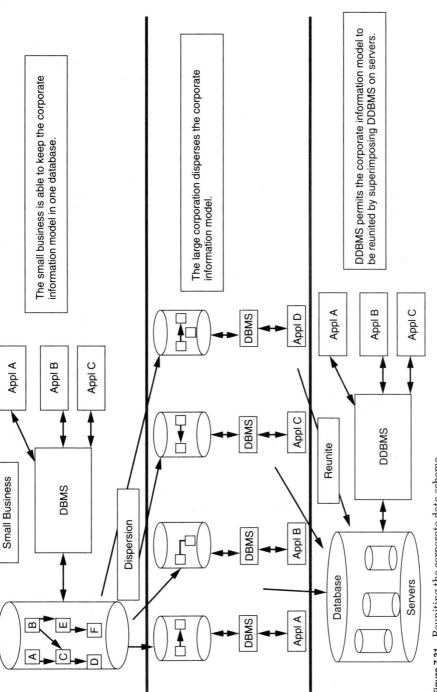

The small business is able to keep the corporate information model in one database.

The large corporation disperses the corporate information model.

DDBMS permits the corporate information model to be reunited by superimposing DDBMS on servers.

Figure 7.31 Reuniting the corporate data schema.

139

- *Section 7.4.1: IM&M Illness Analysis.* Client/server computing, as therapy, will be applied to the four IM&M illnesses. A conclusion will be developed as to its ability to provide symptom, pathology, and/or etiology relief for each illness. The efficacy of client/server computing as a pathology cure for the processing architecture disability will be analyzed by comparing the client/server architecture with the attributes of a powerful architecture (see Table 4.2, "Architecture Attributes").

- *Section 7.4.2: Five Forces Analysis.* Each of the Five Forces and associated factors will be reanalyzed to decide the ability of client/server computing to improve the enterprise maneuverability with respect to each force/factor.

- *Section 7.4.3: Critical Issues Analysis.* Each of the 20 critical issues will be reexamined to decide the degree to which client/server computing enables the achievement of each objective and, consequently, eliminates/minimizes the blocking effect of the illnesses.

Revised impact graphs will be provided to illustrate the qualitative impact of client/server computing on both the Five Forces and the critical issues.

7.4.1   IM&M illness analysis

The purpose of this subsection is to understand the efficacy of client/server computing in treating the IM&M illnesses. Figure 7.32 summarizes the symptoms, pathology, and etiology for each illness that was deduced in Chap. 6. In developing an efficacy judgment for each illness, the following will be provided:

- the illness
- therapeutic effect of client/server computing
- commentary

Client/server computing, as therapy, offers the following relief:

Illness: Processing architecture disability

Therapeutic impact: Cure for pathology of weak architecture

Commentary: Evidence of client/server computing as the pathology cure is best developed by comparing client/server computing with the attributes of a powerful architecture that were summarized in Table 4.2, "Architecture Attributes." Client/server computing meets the requirements of a powerful architecture as follows:

Processing Architecture Disability	Data Disability	Organization Disability	Software Disability
Rigid/Inflexible Systems High Maintenance Costs Fragility of Systems User Dissatisfaction Monolithic Systems Reliance on Obsolete Technologies	Data Mess High Maintenance Costs User Dissatisfaction Reliance on Obsolete Technologies	Proprietary Solutions Tunnel Thinking and Solutions Resistance to Change User Dissatisfaction	Poor Documentation High Maintenance Costs Dependency on Gurus User Dissatisfaction Resistance to Change
Weak Architectures	Dedicated File and Closed Database Architecture	Fortress I/T: Arrogant and Self-Serving	Craft
Immature Discipline	Immature Discipline and Refusal to Adapt Data Engineering Practices	Technology Focus Expediency Strategy	Immature Discipline and Artisan Heritage

Figure 7.32 IM&M illness summary.

- *Maintainability.* The decomposition of monolithic/rigid systems into discrete interlocking parts enhances maintainability. As happens with most engineered products, it is easier to fix/replace/service by constraining repairs to components with well-defined interfaces than to fix/replace/service a single monolithic entity.

- *Modularity.* The client/server architecture is constructed on the notion of connectable modules. Each client and server is a system module which is independently (subject to interfacing constraints) replaceable. New system functions are added by scaling existing modules or adding new modules. New clients are added by scaling existing clients or adding new clients.

- *Adaptability.* Figure 7.3 illustrated the various ways that client/server solutions can distribute presentation, processing, and data services between clients and servers to achieve an initial optimum solution. As circumstances evolve, the partitioning evolves to meet the newer requirements. Recursion (not illustrated) permits endless architectures to be cut and pasted together as solutions. Which mix-and-match set of partitions is best is determined by the application-dependent dimensions of data volume, transaction volume, data manipulation intensity, geographical demographics of users, and attributes of each client/server component.

Figure 7.3 may be understood as follows:

Partition A: Null client / server computing. This is the null case in which all the services are provided in a single processor. The client functions as a display device.

Partition B: Presentation client / server computing. Only presentation services are partitioned to the client. One would anticipate a positive impact relative to traditional host-centered computing on reducing network traffic because, at minimum, the following functions that would have required a complete message flow can now be done locally:

1. screen navigation
2. screen formatting
3. absolute/relative input editing
4. help functions

Partition C: Classical client / server computing. All presentation and processing services are decoupled to the client, and only data services are performed on the server.

Partition D: Hybrid client / server computing. Processing services are placed on both the client and the server.

Partition E: Decoupled client / server computing. Each service is placed on a dedicated client or server machine.

Adaptability is further enhanced by the recursive character of client/server computing that permits the creation of logical services (see Fig. 7.33). A client can request a service of a server that is only a logical service (i.e., through recursion it calls on other servers to do the real work). Highly functional servers can be developed but packaged in endless combinations for simple use by applications. Logical services are the processing equivalent to distributed DBMS, which creates logical databases. By combing the two concepts together, one can create an architecture that is incredibly adaptable since users see only logical services and logical data. The physical services and databases are only accessible through indirection and, consequently, can be reconfigured as required without disturbing the user's view and access to the IM&M world.

Because of this adaptability, client/server computing is robust in configuring an application-driven solution and is equally applicable to both the Business and the About-the-Business Applications. Whether the application is presentation-intensive, processing-intensive, data manipulation-intensive or time-intensive, a solution can be cut and pasted to meet the specific needs.

- *Scalability.* Together with the attributes of modularity, openness/ standards, and adaptability, client/server solutions can be scaled to meet the changing needs of the business. Figure 7.34 provides an example of the scalability of the NCR System 3000 UNIX V/Intel x86 processor line.

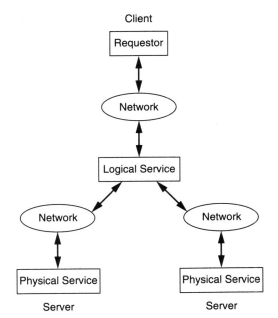

Figure 7.33 Logical services.

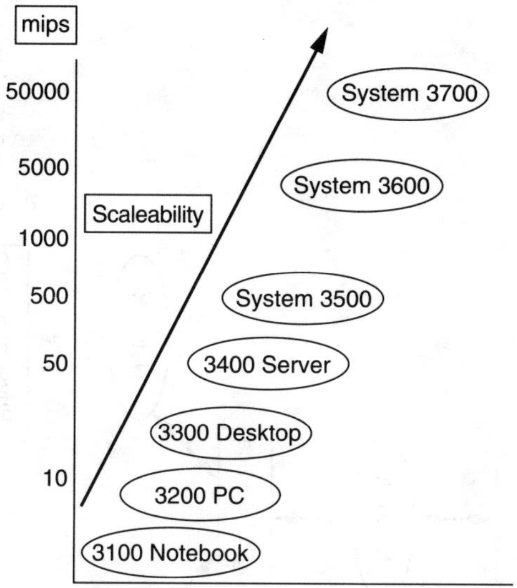

Processor	Role	Comments
3100 – Portable	Portable Client	x386, Notebook Laptop, Pentop, Unix, DOS, OS/2
3200 – Desktop	Entry Client	x386, Unix, DOS, OS/2
3300 – Desktop	Large Client/ Small Server	x386, Unix, DOS, OS/2
3400 – 1–4 Multiprocessors	Local Server	x486, Tightly Coupled Multiprocessors, Unix, DOS, OS/2
3500 – 2–8 Multiprocessors	Regional Server	x486, Mainframe Class, Unix, OS/2
3600 – Medium Parallel	Data Center Server	x486, Loosely Coupled Unix
3700 – Massively Parallel	Data Center Server	x486, Loosely Coupled Unix

Figure 7.34 NCR processor scalability.

- *Portability.* Processing power comes in many sizes: palmtop, note-book, laptop, pentop, desktop, deskside, mainframe, super-mainframe. Building client/server solutions based on standards permits applications to be placed and replaced where it is most advantageous.

- *Openness / standards.* As was discussed in Sec. 7.2, the emergence of IM&M standards was an enabling event to permit the emergence of client/server solutions. Table 7.1 summarizes standards particularly important to client/server computing. As shown in Fig. 7.35, open systems are rapidly obtaining equal functionality with proprietary solutions.

- *Autonomy.* Clients may have minimum capability (as happens with diskless PCs and x-window terminals) or they can be fully configured. Appropriately configured, each client can work both independently and as part of the bonded corporation.

- *Flexibility.* The client/server architecture is a fundamentally stronger architecture to model the real-world complexities of user/computing relationships than is the host-centered model. Figure 7.36 can be used to explain this by referencing basic data-modeling constructs. A one-to-many data-modeling structure permits the modeling of one-to-many relationships (example: a hotel has many rooms). This equates architecturally to the host-centered computing architecture.

  A stronger data-modeling construct is the many-to-many construct that permits the modeling of many-to-many relationships (example: a program is composed of many modules, but a module is included in many programs). This equates to the client/server architecture.

  Just as the many-to-many data-modeling construct is more powerful than the one-to-many construct (because it can better model the complexities of real-world relationships), so a many-to-many architecture (client/server) is more powerful than a one-to-many architecture (host-centered) for the same reason. The one-to-many construct is, in reality, a simple subcase of the many-to-many construct. The many-to-many is the more general case and, consequently, the more flexible one for modeling and revising the system's reflection of the real world.

  A many-to-many construct can model recursive structures (example: a program calls other programs and a program is called by many programs). The recursive capability of client/server computing can analogously model recursive processing structures that the one-to-many architecture cannot.

- *Data accessibility.* Client/server computing enables both the Business and the About-the-Business databases to be positioned as servers. (Section 7.3 discussed this issue in detail.)

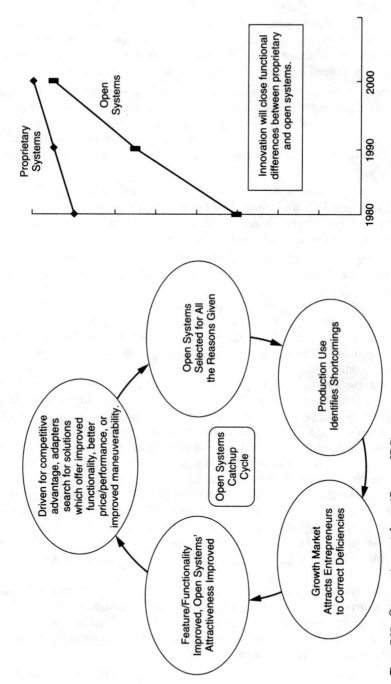

Figure 7.35 Open system catch-up. (*Source: IDC*)

Innovation will close functional differences between proprietary and open systems.

Proprietary Systems

Open Systems

1980   1990   2000

Open Systems Selected for All the Reasons Given

Production Use Identifies Shortcomings

Open Systems Catchup Cycle

Growth Market Attracts Entrepreneurs to Correct Deficiencies

Feature/Functionality Improved, Open Systems' Attractiveness Improved

Driven for competitive advantage, adapters search for solutions which offer improved functionality, better price/performance, or improved maneuverability.

- *Interoperability.* Client/server computing consists of, by definition, clients and servers that are connected over networks. Interoperability is a definition attribute of the architecture.

- *Appliance connectivity.* Information collection, presentation and preparation devices are clients. As long as they meet the bonding requirements, they can be appended to the architecture the same as any other client module.

Client/server computing meets the requirement of a maneuverable architecture. It effectively treats the pathology of the processing architecture disability and, by doing so, broadens the reach and range of the IM&M resource (see Fig. 3.5, "Reach and Range").

Illness: Software disability

Therapeutic impact: Symptom relief

Commentary: Client/server computing provides relief for some major symptoms of the software disability illness. It alleviates the following problems:

- It can reduce maintenance cost because applications inherit the attributes of the architecture that they are built upon. Applications become more scalable, portable, adaptable, modular, etc. All of this, of course, makes it easier to revise the applications in response to the changing business situation.

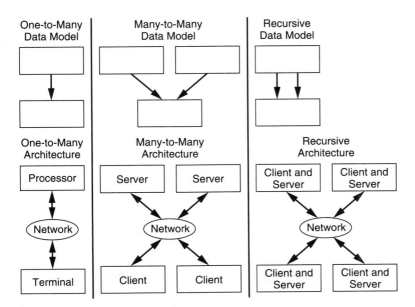

Figure 7.36   Many-to-many architecture.

- It can reduce development costs by permitting an appropriately scaled development environment, different than the target production environment. Software development, as an application, accrues the same flexibility benefits as does any other business application.
- It can improve software productivity by eliminating or minimizing the need to develop new software. As illustrated in Fig. 7.37, as the portfolio of shareable services increases, the time to build new applications decreases because there is a pool of easily reusable services to bond to.

As beneficial as symptom relief is, client/server computing does not eliminate the pathology nor the etiology. Other strategies such as CASE, RAD, object-oriented, etc. need to be adopted to attack this problem.

Illness: Data disability

Therapeutic impact: Partial pathology treatment

Commentary: Client/server computing is a corequisite for creating the desired subject database and decision support database environments described in Chap. 4, Sec. 4.2, "Data Architecture." Before client/server computing, even if you attempted to create the desired data architecture, there was no enabling processing architecture to permit the application portfolio to access it. Distributed DBMS technology when it is inevitably superimposed on top of database servers, will permit the reunion of the corporate information model.

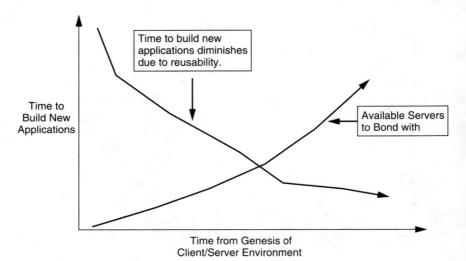

Figure 7.37   Client/server application productivity.

While client/server computing helps, it does not address the etiology of the problem; the absence of proper data administration and data engineering has created a data mess. This critical problem needs to be fully solved and requires the comprehensive implementation of life-cycle data engineering techniques throughout the enterprise.

Illness: Organizational disability

Therapeutic impact: May make worse

Commentary: A successful client/server environment will require:

- data administration
- networking standards
- an information architecture
- standard bonding products with open APIs
- standard software distribution methodologies
- desktop to mainframe design, engineering, and support capabilities (end-to-end service for the users)

Unless IM&M management adapts the precepts of Dr. Deming or another recognized management theorist, the nature of client/server computing will exaggerate and make ever more visible the shortcomings. Distributed, dispersed, or cooperative processing environments require a strong definition of interfacing to make them operable.

Summary.   Client/Server computing vastly improves the IM&M health of the enterprise. It is not a miracle cure for all the illnesses but, as itemized in Table 7.3, it does provide significant treatment for three of the illnesses.

7.4.2   Five Forces analysis

The purpose of this section is to develop an understanding of how client/server computing enables the enterprise to compete more suc-

TABLE 7.3   CSC as Therapy

Client/Server Computing Provides Relief for Three of the Illnesses

IM&M illness	CSC impact
Processing architecture disability	Cures pathology
Software disability	Symptom relief
Data disability	Partial pathology treatment
Organizational disability	Highlights symptoms—may force attention to develop cure

cessfully. This analysis is a complement to the analysis that was done in Chap. 6, Sec. 6.3.1, "Five Forces Analysis." While that analysis was done to assess the degree of IM&M illness, we will now superimpose client/server computing on the Five Forces to learn how it better enables the enterprise to act, react, and adapt to the competitive dynamics.

For each of the Five Forces, the following presentation format will be used:

- The factor
- The original primary affecting illness
- Client/server effect on factor
- Commentary

At the completion of each force analysis, a revised impact graph will be presented that visualizes the improvement in competitive capability due to adoption of client/server computing. (Please refer to Chap. 3, "Business Competition," for a comprehensive review of the Five Forces and associated factors.)

Force 1: Supplier Power. The power of the industry suppliers to control prices, quality, and overall conditions of purchase of goods and services.

- *Factor:* Concentration of suppliers

  Affecting illness: Organization disability

  CSC impact: Positive

  Commentary: The migration to open systems permits mixing and matching vendors and continuous infusion of new products/services from most advantageous supplier.

- *Factor:* Product differentiation

  Affecting illness: Organization disability and software disability

  CSC impact: Positive

  Commentary: Interoperability, open systems, and well-rounded IM&M professionals (due to working with diverse technologies) reduces dependence on embedded supplier.

- *Factor:* Switching costs

  Affecting illness: Processing architecture disability

  CSC impact: Positive

  Commentary: Plug-and-play character of client/server computing reduces switching cost for buyer. Suppliers motivated to compete on price/performance, service, quality, and innovation. Modular nature of client/server architecture permits gradual change as opposed to monolithic change.

- *Factor:* Substitute products

  Affecting illness: Processing architecture disability

  CSC impact: Positive

  Commentary: Open systems, standards, interoperability, etc. all increase options for customer.

- *Factor:* Customer Bypass

  Affecting illness: Not applicable

- *Factor:* Importance of customer to supplier

  Affecting illness: Processing architecture disability

  CSC impact: Positive

  Commentary: Client/server computing reduces dependence of customer on supplier due to elimination of proprietary lock-in. Bargaining power shifts to customer from vendor.

Supplier Power summary. Of the six factors that compose the Supplier Power Force, five are positively influenced by client/server computing. Figure 7.38 illustrates the change in effect. Client/server computing clearly improves the ability of the enterprise to accrue competitive advantage relative to its suppliers.

Force 2: Buyer Power. The degree to which the buyer's ability to influence price, quality, and the other terms of purchase gives the buyer an advantageous bargaining position.

- *Factor:* Buyer concentration

  Affecting illness: All

  CSC impact: Positive

  Commentary: Architecture attributes of client/server computing, adaptability, flexibility, modularity, data accessibility, etc. all improve the enterprise's ability to more rapidly deliver novel/innovative products to expanding markets and reduce dependence on few buyers.

- *Factor:* Product is commodity

  Affecting illness: Processing architecture disability and data disability

  CSC impact: Positive

  Commentary: Client/server computing provides enhanced capability to infuse new value-added as products move through value chain.

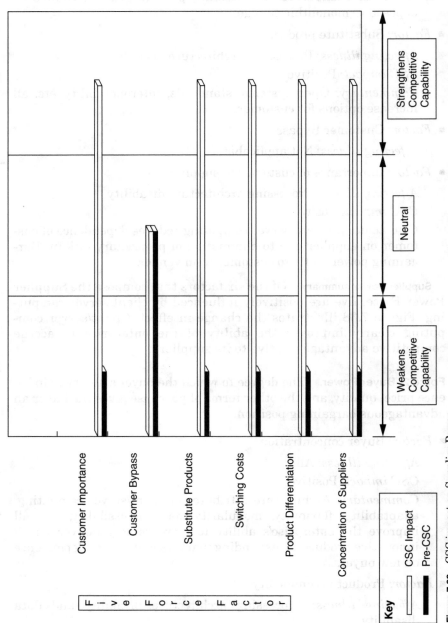

Figure 7.38 CSC impact on Supplier Power.

- *Factor:* Product as component of buyer's cost structure

  Affecting illness: All

  CSC impact: Positive

  Commentary: Client/server computing enables novel ways to reduce cost and improve value of product to customer.

- *Factor:* Buyer profitability

  Affecting illness: Processing architecture disability, data disability, and software disability

  CSC impact: Positive

  Commentary: Bonding to customer's value chain can improve customer's operations, infuse new capability in customer's value chain, and result in higher profitability for customer.

- *Factor:* Product's importance to customer

  Affecting illness: Processing architecture disability, data disability, and software disability

  CSC impact: Positive

  Commentary: Use client/server computing to imbue products with irresistible functionality and service.

- *Factor:* Supplier bypass

  Affecting illness: Processing architecture disability, data disability, and software disability

  CSC impact: Positive

  Commentary: Client/server architecture permits rapid adaptation to customer needs with unique services. Services not available when bypassing you.

Buyer Power summary. Of the seven factors that compose the Buyer Power Force, all are positively influenced by client/server computing. Figure 7.39 illustrates the change. Client/server computing improves the ability of the enterprise to compete relative to its customers.

Force 3: Threat of Entry. The threat that new entrants will join the marketplace and compete for market share.

- *Factor:* Economies of scale

  Affecting illness: Not applicable

- *Factor:* Product differentiation

  Affecting illness: All

  CSC impact: Positive

  Commentary: Use client/server computing to imbue products with irresistible functionality and service, and raise barriers to entry.

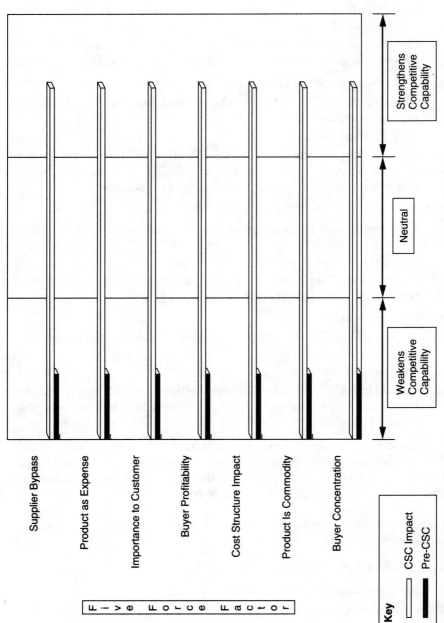

Figure 7.39 CSC impact on Buyer Power.

- *Factor:*   Customer switching costs

  Affecting illness: All

  CSC impact: Positive

  Commentary: Imbue products with features and services that make it impossible for customer to procure elsewhere.

- *Factor:*   Distribution channel access

  Affecting illness: Processing architecture disability

  CSC impact: Positive

  Commentary: Use client/server computing to bond with distributors and raise barriers of entry.

- *Factor:*   Government policy

  Affecting illness: Not applicable

- *Factor:*   Retaliation of incumbents

  Affecting illness: All

  CSC impact: Positive

  Commentary: Use client/server computing to demonstrate ability to react and defend markets.

- *Factor:*   Capital requirements

  Affecting illness: Not applicable

- *Factor:*   Non-economy-of-scale advantages

  Affecting illness: Data disability

  CSC impact: Positive

  Commentary: Use IM&M systems as the ultimate barrier to entry—a swift, agile, and completely adaptable competitor. Who would want to compete?

Threat of Entry summary.   Of the eight factors that compose the Threat of Entry Force, five are positively influenced by client/server computing. Figure 7.40 illustrates the change in effect. Client/server computing clearly improves the ability of the enterprise to compete relative to creating barriers to market entry.

Force 4: Substitute Products.   The existence of substitute products that constrain the ability of the enterprise to control pricing, quality and other factors of sale since there is a point at which the customer will switch.

- *Factor:*   Strong substitute

  Affecting illness: All

  CSC impact: Positive

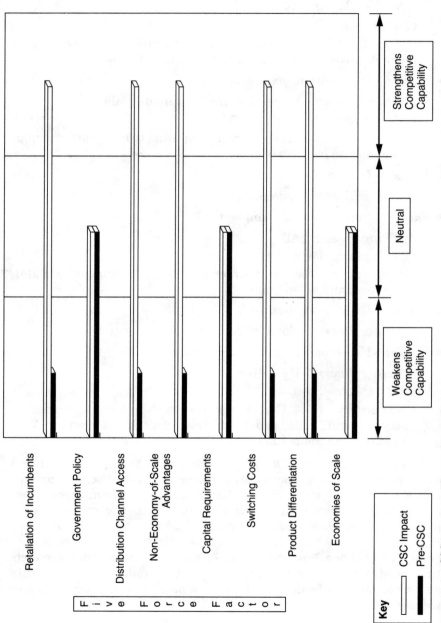

Figure 7.40 CSC impact on Threat of Entry Power.

Commentary: Client/server computing enables the rapid changing of products, services, and features. Provides a moving target for substitutes.

■ *Factor:*   Substitute price/performance trends

Affecting illness: All

CSC impact: Positive

Commentary: Use client/server computing to reengineer value-chain and radically reduce costs.

■ *Factor:*   Profitability of substitute product industry

Affecting illness: Not applicable

■ *Factor:*   Competitive rivalry of substitute product industry

Affecting illness: Not applicable

CSC impact: Positive

Commentary: Higher barriers to entry due to client/server solutions make industry less attractive for other industry players.

Substitute Product summary.   Of the four factors that compose the Substitute Product Force, three are positively influenced. Figure 7.41 illustrates the effect. Client/server computing clearly improves the ability of the enterprise to compete relative to combating substitute products.

Force 5: Rivalry of Existing Competitors.   The degree to which existing competitors battle for market share.

■ *Factor:*   Number and equality of competitors

Affecting illness: All

CSC impact: Positive

Commentary: Client/server computing enables rapid action and reaction to competitors.

■ *Factor:*   Market growth

Affecting illness: Data disability

CSC impact: Positive

Commentary: Use client/server computing to analyze data in novel ways in order to develop new markets and products.

■ *Factor:*   Product differentiation

Affecting illness: All

CSC impact: Positive

Commentary: Use client/server computing to differentiate product throughout value chain.

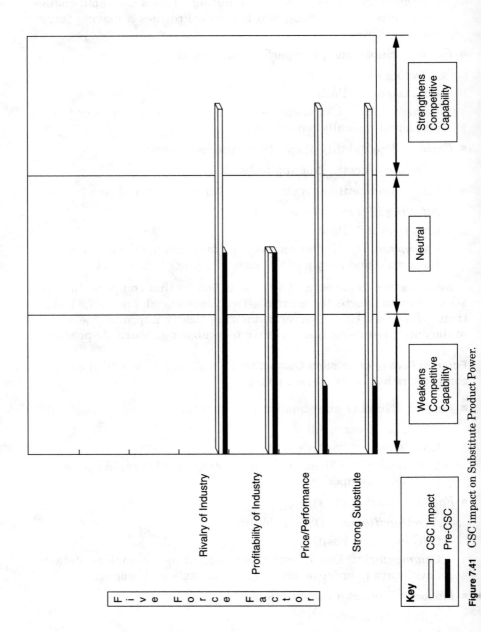

Figure 7.41 CSC impact on Substitute Product Power.

- *Factor:*   Customer switching costs

  Affecting illness: All

  CSC impact: Positive

  Commentary: Deter switching by infusing product with unique services.

- *Factor:*   Fixed costs

  Affecting illness: All

  CSC impact: Positive

  Commentary: Use client/server computing to reduce costs throughout value-chain.

- *Factor:*   Unit of capacity increment

  Affecting illness: Not applicable

- *Factor:*   Exit barriers

  Affecting illness: Not applicable

- *Factor:*   Diversity of corporate personalities

  Affecting illness: Data disability

  CSC impact: Positive

  Commentary: Use client/server computing to improve competitive analysis systems.

Rivalry of Existing Competitors summary.   Of the eight factors that compose the Rivalry Force, six are positively influenced. Figure 7.42 illustrates the change in effect. Client/server computing clearly enables the enterprise to more effectively compete with its rivals.

Five Force analysis summary.   The following conclusions are warranted from this analysis:

- Except for those factors that are not IM&M influenced, CSC has a positive effect on every factor.

- Since processing architecture disability is not the only pathology affecting the Five Forces, client/server computing does not completely solve the problems. Nevertheless, it substantially improves competitive adaptability.

- The previous conclusion is not surprising. As was concluded in Chap. 3, competition demands maneuverability, and client/server computing has been demonstrated to be a maneuverability architecture.

The constant struggle that business engages in is the Five Force struggle for competitive superiority. Client/server computing has been demonstrated to improve the capability of the enterprise to win the struggle.

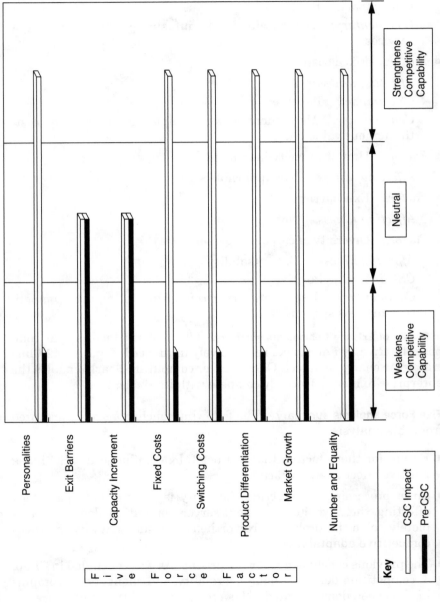

Figure 7.42 CSC impact on Rivalry of Existing Competitors Power.

7.4.3   Critical issues analysis

The purpose of this section is to develop an understanding of how client/server computing enables the achievement of the critical issues objectives. This analysis is a complement to the analysis that was done in Chap. 6, Sec. 6.3.2, "Critical Issues Analysis." While that analysis was done to assess the degree of IM&M illness, we will now review the critical issues to assess the ability of client/server computing to enable their rapid achievement.

For each critical issue, the following presentation format will be used:

- The issue
- The original primary affecting illness
- Client/server impact
- Commentary

At the completion of the analysis, a revised set of impact graphs will be presented that visualizes the enabling capability due to adoption of client/server computing. (Refer to Chap. 5 for a comprehensive review of the issues.)

- *Issue 1:*   Reshape business practices through information technology

  Affecting illness: All

  CSC impact: Positive

  Commentary: CSC provides the required "maneuverable" architecture to reengineer upon.

- *Issue 2:*   Aligning corporate and information system goals

  Affecting illness: Organization disability

  CSC impact: Positive

  Commentary: CSC permits improved access to data, sharing of resources, modular adoption of new technology, and use of application-specific information appliances.

- *Issue 3:*   Instituting cross-functional systems

  Affecting illness: Processing architecture disability and data disability

  CSC impact: Positive

  Commentary: CSC provides required architecture for multiapplication accessing/sharing of subject databases and decision-support databases.

- *Issue 4:*   Boosting software development productivity

  Affecting illness: Software disability

  CSC impact: Positive

Commentary: CSC improves software productivity by: (1) creating reusable services, (2) providing a scaleable/flexible development platform, and (3) providing positive inheritable characteristics to the applications.

■ *Issue 5:*   Utilizing data

Affecting illness: Data disability

CSC impact: Positive

Commentary: CSC provides the necessary accessing architecture to share subject and decision-support databases. (See Sec. 7.3 for a complete discussion.)

■ *Issue 6:*   Developing an information systems strategic plan

Affecting illness: organization disability

CSC impact: Not applicable

■ *Issue 7:*   Improving software development quality

Affecting illness: Processing architecture disability and software disability

CSC impact: Positive

Commentary: Architecture attributes of client/server computing, adaptability, flexibility, modularity, data accessibility, etc. all improve the enterprise's ability to more rapidly deliver software to users by cutting-and-pasting services that already work rather than new development.

■ *Issue 8:*   Creating an information architecture

Affecting illness: All

CSC impact: Positive

Commentary: Client/server computing provides processing architecture component.

■ *Issue 9:*   Integrating information systems

Affecting illness: Processing architecture disability

CSC impact: Positive

Commentary: Interoperability is a basic architectural attribute of client/server computing.

■ *Issue 10:*   Improving leadership skills in information systems

Affecting illness: Not applicable

■ *Issue 11:*   Cutting information systems cost

Affecting illness: All

CSC impact: Positive

Commentary: Life-cycle maneuverability of client/server computing minimizes maintenance costs and encourages reusability.

■ *Issue 12:*   Using information systems for competitive breakthrough

Affecting illness: All

CSC impact: Positive

Commentary: Client/server architecture permits rapid adaptation to customer needs with emergent technologies.

■ *Issue 13:*   Improving the information systems human resource

Affecting illness: Organizational disability

CSC impact: Neutral

■ *Issue 14:*   Educating management on information systems

Affecting illness: Not applicable

■ *Issue 15:*   Connecting to customers and suppliers

Affecting illness: Processing architecture disability and data disability

CSC impact: Positive

Commentary: Interconnect to each other as client and servers.

■ *Issue 16:*   Managing changes caused by information technology

Affecting illness: Not applicable

■ *Issue 17:*   Promoting the information systems function

Affecting illness: All

CSC impact: Positive

Commentary: While client/server computing will visibly improve information systems capability, it will make the other disabilities more glaring.

■ *Issue 18:*   Determining the value of information systems

Affecting illness: Not applicable

■ *Issue 19:*   Managing dispersed systems

Affecting illness: All

CSC impact: Positive

Commentary: CSC provides the required architecture to interconnect the islands of data and processing throughout the enterprise.

■ *Issue 20:*   Capitalize on advances in information technology

Affecting illness: Processing architecture disability

CSC impact: Positive

Commentary: Client/server computing enables the incremental addition of new technology due to its modular character.

Critical issues analysis summary.   The following conclusions are warranted from this analysis:

- The ability to achieve the critical objectives is markedly enabled by CSC. Fourteen of the twenty issues are positively influenced.

- Not surprisingly, a "maneuverable" architecture correlates positively with achievement of business goals.

- If the blockage is to be completely eliminated, action is required to address the other disabilities.

Figures 7.43, 7.44, and 7.45 illustrate the change that client/server computing has in achieving the objectives.

7.4.4   Summary

This section has thoroughly developed the competitive advantages of client/server computing. The following conclusions are warranted:

- The ability to act, react, and maneuver in response to the business dynamics is clearly improved by client/server computing.

- The IM&M illnesses are treated at both the symptom and pathology levels.

- The ability to accomplish the critical issues is effectively deblocked by client/server computing.

What is the superior alternative? What is the counterstrategy? You can do nothing and let entropy grow exponentially as processing dispersion expands in response to computing economics and downsizing feature/function attractiveness. You can continue with terminal emulation as your cooperative processing strategy and place a bandage on the IM&M illnesses. You can halt the drive for interoperability at file servers and achieve limited performance and integrity. What is the prudent choice?

7.5   Conclusions

One can approach change with fear and trepidation or enthusiasm for the opportunities presented. It is not uncommon, unfortunately, for many IM&M industry pundits, experts, gurus, soothsayers, and oracles to sell fear rather than opportunity. Seminars, articles, and briefings by the professional advice givers shout:

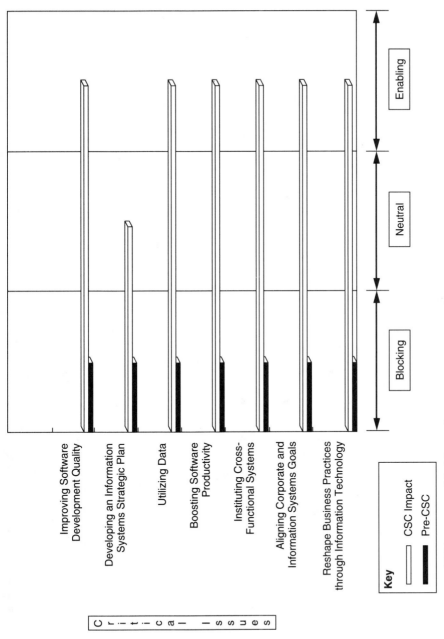

Figure 7.43 CSC impact on critical issues I.

Critical Issues

Improving Software
Development Quality

Developing an Information
Systems Strategic Plan

Utilizing Data

Boosting Software
Productivity

Instituting Cross-
Functional Systems

Aligning Corporate and
Information Systems Goals

Reshape Business Practices
through Information Technology

Blocking   Neutral   Enabling

Key

CSC Impact

Pre-CSC

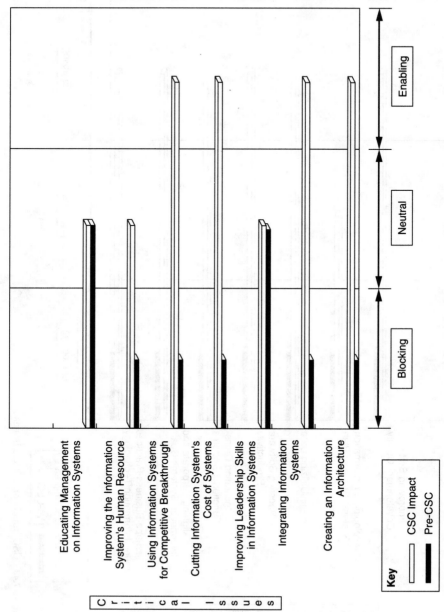

Figure 7.44 CSC impact on critical issues II.

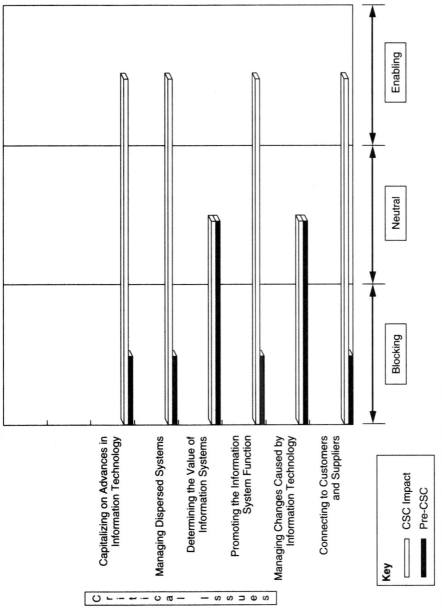

Figure 7.45 CSC impact on critical issues III.

Critical Issues

- Capitalizing on Advances in Information Technology
- Managing Dispersed Systems
- Determining the Value of Information Systems
- Promoting the Information System Function
- Managing Changes Caused by Information Technology
- Connecting to Customers and Suppliers

Blocking   Neutral   Enabling

Key
☐ CSC Impact
■ Pre-CSC

"Mainframe programmers react like Luddites to CSC!"

"Will you 'rightsize' downsize?"

"Network computing: A fad???"

"New problems caused by desktop-centered computing."

"CSC: A risky undertaking?"

"CSC: Is it safe yet?"

"Will you be able to migrate to CSC?"

Over the past 20 years, you could have substituted relational DBMS, fourth-generation languages, CASE, AI, or any other opportunistic technology for CSC in the above list and the warnings would have been roughly the same. Change is to be feared, not seized. It is as though the IM&M manager is a modern-day Odysseus returning from Troy to Ithaca and the vendors are dangerous sirens whose alluring-but-dangerous songs will cause the manager havoc unless he is restrained by the industry pundits. (See Fig. 7.46.)

My advice is simple, unambiguous, and optimistic. You can't learn about, plan for, and implement client/server computing fast enough. The only thing better than implementing it tomorrow would be having implemented it yesterday. What you don't need is the advice of the Cas-

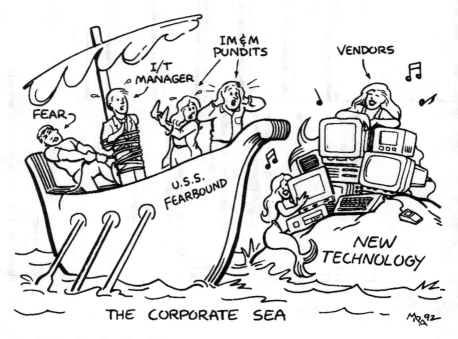

Figure 7.46 A modern-day Odysseus.

sandras of Doom and Gloom who make every challenge twice as difficult. Of course it's hard. Of course it's difficult. What did you expect? Did you have reason to believe that change, suddenly, would be easy? What you require in lieu of pessimism is long-term vision, a plan, and commitment. In the words of Sun Tzu:

> What everyone knows is what has already happened or become obvious. What everyone knows is not called wisdom . . . what the aware individual knows is what has not yet taken shape, what has not yet occurred . . .
>
> If you see the subtle and notice the hidden so as to seize victory where there is not form, this is really good*

Sustainable competitive advantages cannot be built on what is visible to all when it is obvious to all. It is, unfortunately, as visible and obvious to your competitor as it is to you. Opportunity requires vision, not fear, when "there is no form."

What is a worthy vision for the IM&M manager in the 1990s? The IM&M manager should imagine a very different world than currently exists. A world of tremendously powerful workstations (fixed and untethered) with full multimedia support. Processing needs and data are readily available as logical services built on logical servers and distributed DBMS. High-speed networks enable the dispersed enterprise and the customer/supplier-connected enterprise to be bonded as one continuous organism. The enterprise is event-driven: adjusting and correcting itself in response to external stimuli. All kinds of specialized and customized processors and information appliances are appended to the environment to match solutions with business capability requirements. Such a world will be the fifth wave of computing—logical computing (see Fig. 7.2, "Technology Waves")—and is built upon the fourth-wave client/server step.

Client/server computing is not a fad or temporary aberration. The world will not return to the old comforts of host-centered processing. It is not a fad, because it meets an enduring business need: the endless need for advantage. It satisfies the need more economically, with superior feature/functionality and unprecedented adaptability. It alters the tension of the Five Forces Model in favor of the buyer at the expense of the supplier. Client/server computing is not an alluring-but-dangerous song of a technology siren, but a remarkable opportunity to address business problems in novel and imaginative ways.

---

* *The Art of War,* by Sun Tzu.

8

Implementing Client/Server Computing

The purpose of this chapter is to provide IM&M management with insight into the issues that surround a thorough implementation of client/server computing. While the details of an implementation plan and associated projects are highly organization-dependent, there are major issues that transcend specific organizations, and their analysis can aid the individual IM&M manager in developing a comprehensive approach.

It is important to start climbing the client/server learning curve as soon as possible. Figure 8.1 illustrates the variant adoption styles of different organizations. Competitive advantage has three dimensions: development, sustaining, and compounding. Early adapters and scouts have a clear opportunity to gain long-term advantage by the early introduction of new technology. This is because of compounding: newer advantages can be built on existing advantages, and so on and so on. It is not unlike compound interest. If two people invest the same amount of money only 2 years apart at 10 percent per annum, after 5 years the first investor has a 12.5 percent greater return, but after 10 years the difference is about 21 percent. Unless the late investor takes on significantly more risk, he or she will never catch up and, to the contrary, will keep falling farther behind. There is little advantage to be obtained by "riding with the herd."

The journey involved in implementing a major change such as client/server computing should not be underestimated. As Machiavelli understood 500 years ago:

> It should be borne in mind that there is nothing more difficult to handle,
> nor more doubtful of success, and more dangerous to carry through than

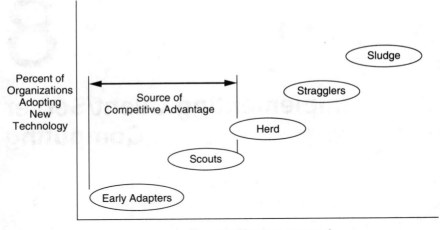

Figure 8.1   Organization adaptability.

initiating change. The innovator makes enemies of all those who prospered under the older order, and only lukewarm support is forthcoming from those who would prosper under the new. Their support is lukewarm partly from fear of their adversaries, who have the existing laws on their side, and partly because men are generally incredulous, never really trusting new things unless they have tested them by experience. In consequence, those who oppose the changes attack vigorously and the defense made by the others is only lukewarm.*

The situation with implementing client/server computing is such because the change from host-centered computing to client/server computing (see Fig. 1.5, "Migration of Business Systems Architecture") is a paradigm shift that mandates repositioning many strategic areas of the business (see Table 2.1, "Strategic Areas"). In many ways, the technology shift is the simplest change; the greatest challenge is the realignment of all the other strategic areas in harmony with the new client/server paradigm. They were all aligned with host-centered computing and must all now be repositioned.

Thomas Kuhn understood the challenge of shifting paradigms when he wrote:

. . . paradigm debates are not really about relative problem-solving ability, though for good reasons they are usually couched in those terms. Instead the issue is which paradigm should in the future guide research on problems, many of which neither competitor can yet claim to solve completely. A decision between alternate ways of practicing science is called

---

* *The Prince,* Machiavelli, translated by G. Bull, Penguin Books, 1961.

for, and in those circumstances that decision must be made less on past achievement than on future promise. The man who embraces a new paradigm at an early stage must often do so in defiance of the evidence provided through existing problem solving. He must, that is, have faith that the new paradigm will succeed with the many large problems that confront it, knowing only that the old paradigm has failed with a few. A decision of that kind can only be made on faith.*

Armed with a Machiavellian warning and Kuhn's understanding, the executive must develop a complete plan, understanding full well the obstacles to be confronted.

The remaining sections of this chapter will attempt to alleviate the obstacles and expedite the paradigm shift by analyzing the impact of client/server computing on the other strategic areas. This will be accomplished as follows:

- *Section 8.1: Strategic Planning Model Revisited.*   This section will complete the development of the strategic planning model that was introduced in Chap. 2, Section 2.1, "Strategic Management." Added to the model will be the factors of strategic intent, barrier analysis, and commitment strategy. With this richer model, a complete framework for developing a robust implementation plan will be available.

- *Section 8.2: Repositioning.*   This section will do a thorough analysis of the issues involved in repositioning the enterprise from host-centered computing to client/server computing. Using the 7 "S" Model as a guide, an impact analysis will be made of the repositioning required concerning suppliers, technology, organization structure, human resources, information systems, management systems, and finances. A barrier analysis approach will be developed to aid in anticipating obstacles and planning to overcome them. Alternative approaches to demonstrating commitment to the effort will also be developed.

- *Section 8.3: Conclusion.*   This section will reach conclusions on the major points of this chapter.

At the completion of this chapter, the reader will have an insightful understanding of the underlying issues involved in moving the enterprise from $P_{prior\ client/server}$ to $P_{client/server-computing}$. Paradigm shifts are disruptive events, but highly opportunistic for those who understand them. It is difficult to change position relative to a competitor during times of stability and complacency. Paradigm shifts provide rare opportunities of discontinuous change during which relationships can be radically altered.

---

* *The Structure of Scientific Revolutions,* Thomas Kuhn, The University of Chicago Press, 1970.

8.1 Strategic Planning Revisited

The purpose of this section is to complete the development of the strategic planning model that was initiated in Chap. 2, Section 2.1, "Strategic Management." The completed model provides a richer framework from which to implement client/server computing. The following notions will be appended to the model:

- *Section 8.1.1: Strategic Intent.*   Strategic intent is the long-term ambition of our efforts. It is our vision of the future state of information systems. Strategic intent provides a constancy of long-term purpose in a volatile and often expedient world.

- *Section 8.1.2: Barrier Analysis.*   Barrier analysis is a specific analytical method that is used to develop foreknowledge of obstacles that may block the success of the implementation programs and associated projects. By performing a complete barrier analysis, problems can be anticipated and actions included in the implementation programs to alleviate them.

- *Section 8.1.3: Commitment Strategy.*   The commitment strategy consists of specific actions that the sponsoring executives take to convince the impacted staff that this time management is "serious" about change. It is the up-front planning and execution required to establish credibility for the implementation effort with an often jaded and cynical organization. It addresses the question of "How do you convince the staff that this time management is serious about realigning itself in synchronization with the shifted paradigm?"

A quick review of Fig. 2.1, "Strategic Planning Model I," before starting this chapter is advisable:

- A situational analysis is done on relevant strategic areas (Table 2.1, "Strategic Areas"). Using an assortment of analytical methods, the situation is encapsulated into strengths, weaknesses, opportunities, threats, critical success factors, etc.

- Conclusions are developed on issues requiring specific actions.

- Strategic objectives are presented that define a new, more desirable position. Objectives are specific, dated, and measurable.

- Strategies are developed as the purposeful and coherent actions to move the organization from the current situation to the desired situation.

- Implementation programs, decomposed into projects, are initiated for each strategy to operationalize the repositioning. Projects achieve interim goals on the journey to achieving the objectives.

By the conclusion of this chapter, Fig. 2.1 will be revised as illustrated in Fig. 8.2. This model includes the added notions of strategic intent, barrier analysis, and commitment strategy.

8.1.1   Strategic intent

Strategic intent is the long-term ambition of our efforts. It is the far-reaching and long-term objective that we strive for. It provides constancy and focus of purpose in an increasingly immediate results-oriented world. A worthy strategic intent for implementing client/server computing would be as follows:

> It is our long-term intent, the obsession of our efforts, to put in place an IM&M capability that enables the enterprise to compete effectively through total systems maneuverability. Our IM&M capability will provide the greatest possible reach and range for applications to be developed and evolved upon.

Such an intent is worthy of the travails of a paradigm shift.

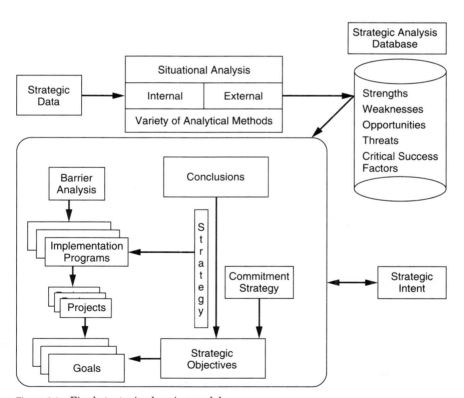

Figure 8.2   Final strategic planning model.

It should now be even clearer why the implementation of client/server computing requires managing in the strategic context. As illustrated in Fig. 8.3, it will take multiple planning cycles to accomplish the intent objective. The strategic planning context provides the long-term constancy and focus of purpose that is required for a multi-period implementation.

8.1.2 Barrier analysis

Barrier analysis is an analytical method used to anticipate and preempt problems in achieving the objectives. It is a planning tool by which one anticipates implementation problems and includes in the implementation programs actions to deal with them. Figure 8.4 illustrates the approach.

Using techniques such as brainstorming, potential barriers are identified and listed across the top of the matrix. A *barrier* is any reasonable obstacle that would block achievement of the implementation programs. Down the side of the matrix are listed each of the implementation programs and the associated projects. An analysis is then made to decide which barriers impact which projects. Intersection cells identify barriers that impede project achievement and are completed with "Resistance Reduction Tactics" to be included in the implementation programs to overcome the barrier.

Barriers may be identified at three levels:

1. *General barriers.* Barriers that are due to organizational history, culture, style, etc.

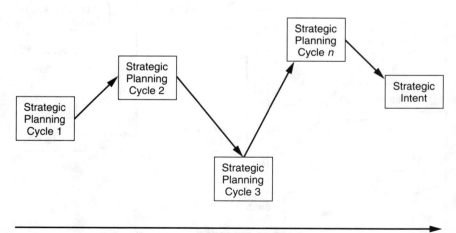

Change in Position Over Time

Figure 8.3 Realizing strategic intent.

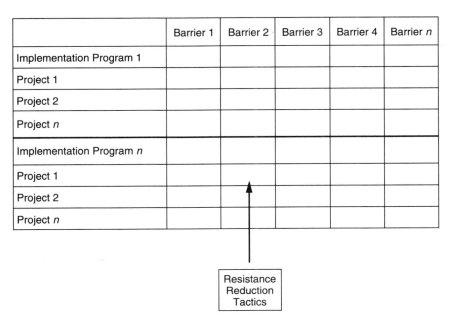

	Barrier 1	Barrier 2	Barrier 3	Barrier 4	Barrier *n*
Implementation Program 1					
Project 1					
Project 2					
Project *n*					
Implementation Program *n*					
Project 1					
Project 2					
Project *n*					

Resistance
Reduction
Tactics

Figure 8.4   Barrier analysis analytical method.

2. *Role barriers.*   Barriers that can be associated with specific incumbent job functions.

3. *Individual barriers*   Specific people of influence who will oppose the effort and therefore cause obstacles.

Different resistance reduction tactics are appropriate for each type. What are the typical barriers that need to be overcome? The following is a good starter list for an IM&M paradigm shift:

- *Partisan warfare.*   The entrenched interest groups fight to protect their territory.

- *Inertia.*   The natural tendency of bureaucracies not to move or, at best, to move slowly. People prefer the status quo.

- *Disbelief.*   People with substantial investments in the existing IM&M technologies will refuse to accept the paradigm shift. They will enter a state of aggressive denial.

- *Expediency culture.*   The organization culture rewards and emphasizes short-term gains, and orderly movement to client/server computing requires a long-term strategic implementation.

- *Positional "misfit."*   The strategic areas are so out of synchronization to support client/server computing that the effort will be Herculean.

- *Fear of failure.*   The reward systems and culture punish risk taking.

- *"It works."*   An attitude that the existing IM&M investment works. Why should we change it?

- *Lack of leadership.*   There is an absence of vision and understanding of the changes taking place.

- *Complacency.*   Change upsets everyone.

- *Competition for limited investment resources.*   Other corporate projects have higher priority.

These are general barriers that have to be dealt with. In each case, the implementation team should brainstorm, and propose specific action plans to deflect them.

Besides the general barriers, certain organizational roles and/or individuals will be identifiable as barriers. For example, the data center operations manager may be opposed to the introduction of open systems into the data center or the DBMS manager may not want to have his or her staff learn new portable DBMS products. In dealing with individuals, responses can be grouped into six categories:

1. *Carrot approach.*   Offer the individual some specific benefit.

2. *Stick approach.*   Provide a viable threat that will dissuade the individual from opposing the effort.

3. *Skip approach.*   Convince the individual's supervisor that the idea is worthy and the individual will be motivated by the hierarchy.

4. *Blitzkrieg approach.*   Move quickly, before the individual can organize any resistance.

5. *Positioning approach.*   Arrange enough supporting factors so that the individual will recognize that opposition is untenable.

6. *Negotiate approach.*   Discuss the issues frankly and attempt to reach a mutually satisfying compromise.

There is a tendency to ignore this step, which we advise against strongly. As Machiavelli warned, change is a difficult undertaking, and you will make enemies of all those who prosper and believe that they can continue to prosper under the old paradigm. The barrier analysis, coupled with the commitment strategy, provides a thoughtful way to deal with this inevitability.

Sun Tzu said: "Those who are good at getting rid of trouble are those who take care of it before it arises."* Through anticipation, barriers can be eliminated and/or minimized.

---

* *The Art of War* by Sun Tzu.

8.1.3   Commitment strategy

A *commitment strategy* is a specific set of actions taken to establish credibility.* A commitment strategy is an action or set of actions designed to alter the beliefs/actions/behaviors of others to motivate desired behaviors. We wish to devise a commitment strategy that will push/pull the organization to voluntarily and enthusiastically reposition itself in harmony with the new client/server paradigm.

It is unfortunate, but the reality is that many management teams have little credibility with the mass of workers. Each year new programs are announced with tremendous fanfare and each year they die a slow death. The staff, understandingly jaded and cynical, reacts with a predictable maxim: "This too shall pass." They suspect that management has few deep beliefs and is committed to even fewer. Because of this and the reality that little is accomplished without the endorsement and efforts of all the people, the inclusion of a commitment strategy to provide and sustain credibility in an expedient world is a necessary part of an implementation program.

A credible commitment strategy can be constructed on three principles as follows:

1. *Alter your own payoff.* The objective of this approach is to rearrange the situation so that it is clearly not in your own interest to alter direction. It becomes clear to all that a reversal is not likely because a reversal is clearly contrary to the management team's own benefit. Two tactical ways to accomplish this are:

   - *Reputation on the line.* Put your reputation clearly and firmly behind the effort.

   - *Contractual obligation.* Be subject to clear penalties for failure to carry through on the effort.

2. *Make it difficult to back out.* The objective of this approach is to constrain your ability to change direction. It makes it visible that you won't change direction because you can't. Four tactical ways to accomplish this are as follows:

   - *Cut off communication.* Literally take yourself out of the loop and thereby prevent a reversal.

   - *Burn your bridges behind you.* Commit an irreversible act that makes accomplishment of the effort mandatory.

   - *Leave the outcome to chance.* Put in place a process that has a life of its own and that you can't control.

---

* The ideas on commitment strategy are based on *Thinking Strategically,* A. Dixit & B. Nalebuff, W.W. Norton & Co., 1991.

- *Small steps.* Proceed in many well-defined and small steps with visible payoffs. Changing direction is deterred because of the remaining payoffs from just "one more step."

3. *Use others to force/maintain commitment.* The objective of this approach is to make it difficult to revise your direction because of the others involved. It alters the belief of the staff because they feel while one person might change, all of them never would. Two tactical ways to accomplish this are as follows:

- *Teamwork.* Get many people in the boat with you. You all have to swim or sink together.

- *Delegated agent.* Delegate authority to someone whose interest is clearly to accomplish the effort. This makes a reversal highly unlikely.

The above are general strategies and need to be customized to the situation. The overall point, however, is clear. To be successful in managing the paradigm shift, it will be necessary for the staff to believe that the management team is thoroughly committed to the transformation. As you will see in the next section, there is a tremendous gap to be crossed in repositioning the organization for client/server computing. The clear commitment of the management team to the effort significantly eases the passage.

8.2   Repositioning

The purpose of this section is to analyze the issues involved in repositioning the organization from $P_{\text{prior client/server computing}}$ to $P_{\text{client/server computing}}$. The idea used to realize this purpose is derived from the 7 "S" Model developed by McKinsey & Co.* The 7 "S" Model suggests that strategy implementation is far more than just the dimensions of strategy and organization structure. Rather, all the strategic areas that are impacted by the strategy have to be realigned as well. McKinsey's 7 "S"s were strategy, structure, systems, style, staff, shared values, and skills. We will enlarge this set to include all the strategic areas listed in Table 2.1.

Figure 8.5 illustrates the realignment concept. As the result of the situational analysis, the organization is in some position relative to its IM&M strategy. That position may be anywhere from *entropic* (all the strategic areas are misaligned with each other) to *harmony* (all the strategic areas are in alignment and complement each other—the ideal), or mixed (some alignment, some misalignment—the normal situation). Successful implementation means moving all the

---

* "The Seven Elements of Strategic Fit," R. Waterman Jr., *Journal of Business Strategy*.

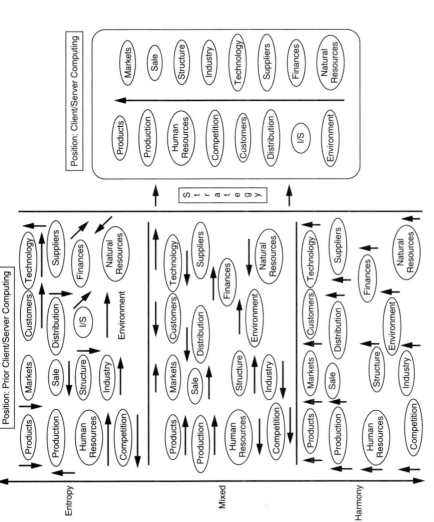

Figure 8.5 Repositioning.

strategic areas into a "strategic fit" with the client/server strategy. This is not a trivial task under normal circumstances but the challenge is even greater given the gross realignment needed because of the paradigm shift.

The remainder of this section will explore the major issues involved in the repositioning. The discussion will be partitioned as follows:

- *Section 8.2.1: The Supplier.* This section will analyze the issues surrounding a revised relationship with IM&M suppliers due to client/server computing. Topics covered will be:

  out-sourcing

  vendor relationship management

  a single client/server supplier

- *Section 8.2.1: Technology.* This section will discuss technology positioning and evaluation issues that are impacted by the implementation of client/server computing. Topics covered will be:

  SQL grafting

  mainframe role in client/server computing

  Advanced technology groups

- *Section 8.2.3: Organization Structure.* This section will discuss how the information technology organization has to be restructured to support client/server computing.

- *Section 8.2.4: Human Resources.* This section will discuss the impact of client/server computing on the information-technology human resource. Issues covered for repositioning will include:

  education/retraining

  core competencies

  values/behavior systems

- *Section 8.2.5: Information Systems.* This section will suggest tactics that can be deployed to support a gradual migration of the embedded application portfolio to the client/server architecture.

- *Section 8.2.6: Management Systems.* This section will discuss changes required to management systems to support the client/server initiative. Topics covered will be:

  strategic planning

  quality

  competitor analysis

  applying IM&M to the IM&M business functions

- *Section 8.2.7: Sustainable Competitive Advantage.* This section will discuss how the implementation of client/server computing can be infused with sustainable competitive advantage (SCA) for the corporation. SCA can be built upon:

inter-LAN and wide area high-speed peer to peer networking capability

configuration management

end-to-end operations, administration, and maintenance capability

- *Section 8.2.8: Repositioning Summary.* This section will summarize the essential points of the discussion.

Strategic planning is the art of managed change. Moving from P_{prior} client/server computing to $P_{client/server computing}$ needs to be done with forethought and appreciation of the total problem. As the 7 "S" Model instructs us, we wish to be repositioned to an elegant strategic fit.

8.2.1   The supplier

There are three issues of strategic fit regarding client/server computing and suppliers. These are:

- *Out-sourcing.* The practice of purchasing all or part of IM&M services from an outside vendor.

- *Vendor partnering.* Engaging in a long-term preferred relationship with a vendor.

- *Single supplier tactic.* Purchasing complete client/server solutions from a single supplier only.

Each will be discussed individually.

Out-sourcing. *Out-sourcing* is the purchasing of a major information technology function/service, which has traditionally been provided by the internal IM&M organization, from an outside vendor. There is a wide continuum of out-sourcing arrangements, ranging from facilities management of the data center as a utility to application development to planning and strategy. Figure 8.6 illustrates the continuum of services that may be out-sourced. The primary rationale for out-sourcing is divided into four categories as follows:

- *Economics.* The vendor, due to economy of scale and expertise, can offer pricing superior to the internal service.

- *Skills / competency.* The vendor has access to a critical mass of talent that is increasingly difficult or expensive to support internally.

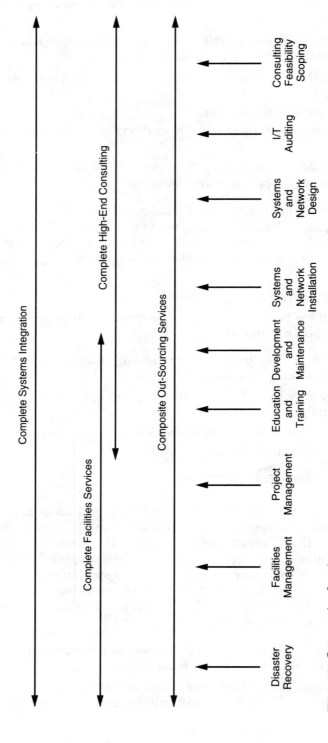

Figure 8.6 Out-sourcing functions.

- *Breadth of resources.*   The vendor, as a complete information-technology supplier, has capabilities beyond those available in-house.

- *Focus.*   The company can focus on its core business (which is not IM&M) and pay the vendor to do what he or she does best. Each can concentrate their resources.

Figure 8.7 illustrates the tremendous growth anticipated for outsourcing.

The question that needs to be asked in light of the asserted importance of IM&M to competitive health in general, and the opportunities presented by client/server computing in particular, is: "Does outsourcing make sense to the client/server opportunistic enterprise?" Should your company join those firms (such as are itemized in Table 8.1) which have opted for the out-sourcing alternative?

To answer that question, we turn again to Machiavelli for counsel:

> . . . the arms on which a prince bases the defense of his state are either his own, or mercenary or auxiliary. Mercenaries and auxiliaries are useless and dangerous. If a prince bases the defense of his state on mercenaries, he will never achieve stability or security . . . the reason for this is that there is no loyalty or inducement to keep them on the field apart from the little they are paid and that is not enough to make them want to die for

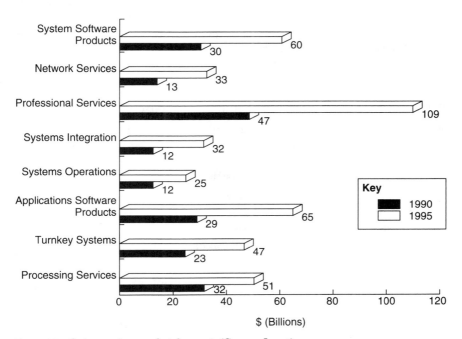

Figure 8.7   Out-sourcing market forecast. (*Source: Input*)

TABLE 8.1   Major Out-Sourcing Contracts

Many Large and Well-Respected Firms Have Chosen Out-Sourcing

Client	Value	Systems integrator
General Dynamics	$3 b	CSC
Continental Airlines	$2.1 b	EDS
Enron Corp.	$750 M	EDS
Continental Bank	$700 M	EDS
First City Bancorp	$600 M	ISSC
Eastman Kodak Co.	$500 M	ISSC
National Car Rental	$500 M	EDS
First Fidelity Bancorp	$450 M	EDS
First American Bancshares Inc.	$400 M	Perot Systems

you . . . I conclude, therefore, that unless it commands its own arms, no principality is secure, rather it is dependent on fortune since there is no valor and no loyalty to defend it when adversity comes."*

Machiavelli's basic thesis is that the defense of the state was critical to its survival and that such a fundamental capability should not be "out-sourced" to mercenaries. The essential truth and insight of Machiavelli's analysis is equally valid regarding out-sourcing today. If IM&M is so critical an enabling capability to the enterprise, and client/server computing will offer such opportunities for competitive advantage, why would you jeopardize the welfare of your state and out-source it to those "with no valor and no loyalty"? Are short-term tactical advantages such as immediate cost savings so valuable that the long-term ability to compete should be compromised?

Regarding out-sourcing and client/server computing, we conclude the following:

- Only strict utility functions should be out-sourced.

- Even retention of the strategic and planning functions and out-sourcing the execution is dangerous. Success requires both superior planning and superior execution. A mercenary army at your command is not an advantageous position.

- Most management theorists emphasize, as did Machiavelli, the importance of loyalty, trust, shared values, concern, etc. between the leadership and the doers. Out-sourcing does not build a long-term bond of trust and common objectives between the strategist, the planners, and the ones who execute.

- The jury is still out. Despite all the attention given out-sourcing in the last few years, the game is only in the first inning. Strategic mis-

---

* *The Prince,* Machiavelli.

takes, as well as strategic victories, take time to become visible. We must wait a few years to see what becomes of the out-sourced organizations versus those that invested in internal capabilities and competent staffs.

I conclude with a clear position on this topic. In light of the almost unbelievable opportunity that information technology in general, and client/server computing in particular, offers the enterprise, out-sourcing (except for utility functions) doesn't appear even to make good nonsense. While this is obviously a dissident position in light of the major out-sourcing arrangements that have been announced in the airline, lodging, and financial industries, I take refuge in the following:

- As stated before, the jury is still out. Don't confuse the glitter and fanfare of the announcement with success five years later.

- Several articles are beginning to be circulated from academia which show that the real motivation for out-sourcing is short-term financial gain. There is nothing wrong with that, but short-term financial gain is not long-term strategic competitive advantage.

- Consider the advisers. Machiavelli has been referenced for 500 years and will most likely be referenced for another 500. The typical out-sourcing proponent is 40 years old and will be forgotten rather quickly. This is not to suggest that times don't change and that advice must be reconsidered in light of changed circumstances, but the basic notion of Machiavelli's advice remains cogent. One should not surrender to others those capabilities that are vital to your well being. IM&M is such a capability.

Time will be the best judge whether out-sourcing results in competitive advantage or mediocrity.

Vendor partnering. Vendor partnering refers to a developing practice whereby, rather than the traditional adversarial way vendors and customers relate to each other (with guarded suspicion and distrust), they partner together on a long-term basis to continually improve the quality of the product/service. One of the leading advocates of this practice is Dr. W. E. Deming who, in his 14 points, suggests ". . . that you move toward a single supplier for any one item on a long-term relationship of loyalty and trust."* Vendors should be selected for the long haul, and the relationship based on value and quality, not initial cost.

Vendor partnering is a particularly relevant topic for client/server computing because, as we will discuss later, the IM&M organization

---

* *Out of the Crisis,* Dr. W. Edwards Deming.

shifts from being a parts supplier to being a systems integrator. Obviously, the ability to integrate components from multiple suppliers in a timely manner is bounded by:

- the quality of the received components
- the number of components that have to be integrated
- the ability to manage/plan change in an orderly manner

Client/server computing will require the IM&M organization to become an end-to-end integrator: from desktop to mainframe. The partnering concept is extremely attractive as a way to:

- constantly improve quality
- minimize the number of parts and permutations that have to be integrated
- coordinate new releases

At the same time, however, the Five Forces Model views the relationship between supplier and buyer as adversarial. Porter suggests:

> - Increase bargaining power in purchasing by keeping the number of sources sufficient to insure competition, but small enough to be an important buyer to each source.
> - Select suppliers who are especially competitive with each other and divide purchasing among them.
> - Vary the proportions of business awarded to suppliers over time to insure that they do not view it as an entitlement.*

What are we to do? How do we deal with and explain the paradox?

The dilemma is explained by understanding what, in game theory, is called the *Prisoners Dilemma*. The Prisoners Dilemma refers to a situation where, by attempting to optimize their own payoffs, individual game players receive less than if they would "trust and cooperate with each other." The dilemma of course is the problem of trust.

Figure 8.8 illustrates the situation. Both the buyer and the supplier can execute one of two strategies: be either a "Deming Partner" or a "Five Force Antagonist." The number in the top right of each cell gives the buyer payoff and the number in the lower-left corner of each cell gives the supplier payoff for the convergence of strategies in that cell. Both the buyer and supplier have what is referred to in game theory as a *dominant strategy*. A dominant strategy is a strategy that gives the best relative payoff no matter what the opponent does. For both players, the dominant strategy is Five Force Antagonist and the game ends

---

* *Competitive Advantage,* Dr. Michael Porter.

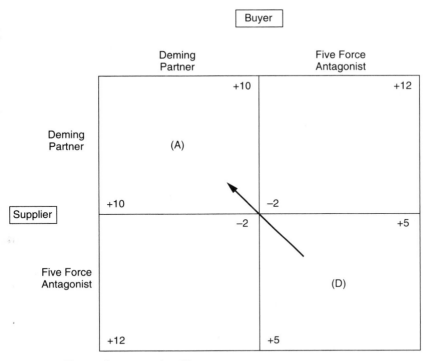

Figure 8.8   The vendor partnering dilemma.

in cell "D." The dilemma of course is that if they would trust and cooperate with each other and engage in the Deming Partner strategy, they
would each get a mutually superior payoff (cell "A"). Of course if either
cheated, that individual would get a maximum payoff and the other
would take a big loss. Trust does not come easily.

So we have the problem. Both Deming and the Five Forces are right;
they simply make very different assumptions about the behaviors of
the players. It would unquestionably be advantageous to engage in
"Deming Partnering," but how do we protect ourselves from cheating?
If we are to move beyond Five Force Antagonist, advantage can only be
accrued by mutual trust and respect. How is this to occur?

In *Thinking Strategically,** four suggestions are given on how to
escape the dilemma, achieve cooperation, and achieve the superior
mutual payoff:

- Establish a way to detect cheating.
- Establish punishments for cheating.

---

* *Thinking Strategically* by Dixit and Nalebuff.

- Establish frequent periodic reviews for the purpose of deciding whether to continue the relationship. The cheater would be confronted with a small short-term gain and a significant long-term loss.
- The punishment should be clear, sizable, and doable.

In summary:

- Vendor partnering is a desirable component of repositioning to support the client/server environment.
- Vendor partnering requires unprecedented cooperation between the buyer and supplier to achieve the mutually superior payoff.
- Include the above approaches in the partnering arrangement to detect and punish cheating.

Since vendor partnering is so alien, start small, gain acceptance, and evolve.

Single supplier. Some industry consultants strongly recommend *sole-sourcing* for implementing client/server solutions. While this would superficially appear to be the ultimate form of vendor partnering, the intention and motivation are quite different. Their concern is that, given the emerging state of client/server computing technology, the transition/adoption problems will be minimized by dealing with a single supplier. The hope is that solutions from a single supplier will be preintegrated and thereby eliminate integration hurdles for the customer.

While this is a prudent tactical way to commence the learning/experience process, it should not be confused with the ultimate objective. A single supplier for all client/server needs would be disadvantageous from several perspectives.

- No single supplier will provide all the required information appliances.
- All the suppliers that you wish to connect with may not be using your IM&M supplier.
- All the customers that you will want to connect with may not be using your IM&M supplier.
- Specialized servers that are advantageous for you may not be provided by the single supplier.
- The ultimate benefit of open systems, portability, scalability, and interoperability is freedom to pick and choose. Why give up the most precious benefit of the architecture?

While using a single supplier as an initial kick-off strategy is a reasonable thing to do, such a long-term approach is counterproductive and defeats the fundamental benefits of the client/server architecture.

8.2.2 Technology

The purpose of this section is to analyze the major repositioning issues with regard to the technology dimension. The issues that will be covered are as follows:

- *SQL grafting.* The prospect of accelerating migration to the client/server architecture by superimposing (grafting) an SQL data manipulation language on the huge embedded base of network and hierarchical databases.

- *The mainframe role.* The repositioning of the mainframe within the client/server environment.

- *Advanced technology groups.* The creation of technology assessment groups to assess new technology, link it to business practices and capabilities, and integrate it into existing IM&M products/services.

Each will be discussed separately.

SQL grafting. Given the large embedded base of hierarchical and network databases that are operational, an extremely desirable migration technology would be the "grafting" of an SQL interface onto existing hierarchical/network databases (see Fig. 8.9). Such a data manipulation language would enable new applications to operate against our database heritage but without the time/cost of conversion. New rela-

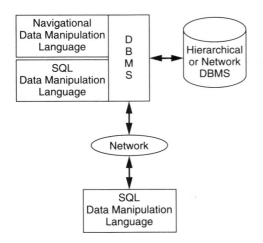

Figure 8.9 SQL grafting.

tional applications could then be developed (including client/server SQL access) while the embedded base continues operating undisturbed.

Several vendors are promising such "lead-into-gold" interfaces. Such a technology would expedite the repositioning, but is it a worthwhile investment of time and effort or is it fool's gold? Several excellent analysis papers indicate inherent and fundamental contradictions in delivering such a technology except, in trivial situations. For example:

- How would SQL handle overlapping fields?
- How would SQL handle multi-identity fields?
- How would SQL handle essential ordering rules?
- How would SQL join records/segments that are pointer-related but have no common keys?
- How would "insert" work when the insert rule is "here, next, prior, or first"?
- How would SQL handle multirecord sets?

All in all, while clearly desirable, there is unfortunately much reason for skepticism and a low probability of success.

Even without those problems, if for the sake of argument we assumed they are solved, the total illogic of what is being proposed from a performance perspective needs to be understood. Traditional hierarchical and network databases were not designed for general purpose and/or unstructured access. To the contrary, they were carefully designed for engineered access. Generally, hierarchical and network databases went through the following development sequence (see Fig. 8.10):

- *Logical design.* A logical, normalized data model was developed along with a set of logical access transactions. The two were bounced against each other to see that all transactions could be met by the database.
- *Physical design.* Given the physical design options of the chosen DBMS (indexes, sets, hashing, clustering, etc.), a physical design for the database is iterated. Explicit physical access strategies are developed for each transaction. The combined physical database design and physical access strategies are explicitly designed to perform at some level. No claims are made about any other transactions.
- *Database sizing.* The database is sized for the given design based on start-up volumes and anticipated growth. An unacceptable size will result in going back to the previous step for a new design. Sizing also includes the design of the DBMS "system generation" options

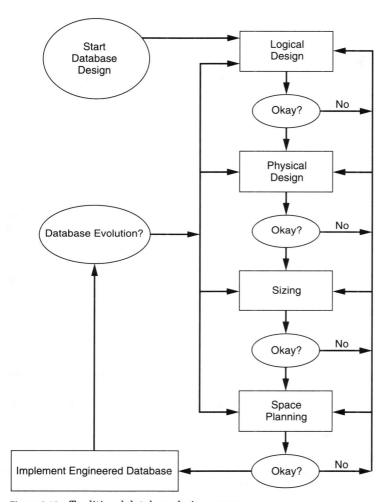

Figure 8.10 Traditional database design process.

that are database tunable. Examples of this would include sizing of internal buffers, mapping of database files to buffers, buffer residency priorities, and number of locking pools.

- *Space planning.*   A space plan is developed to spread the sized database over the physical hardware configuration of the target processing environment. This planning considers channel input/output balancing, placement on disk strings, and (if possible) explicit placement of database files on specific parts of disks to minimize read/write movement. The physical transaction access plans are again bounced against the combined physical database design and space plan to assure engineered performance.

- *Evolution.* When changes occur (new transactions, growth in database size, schema change, etc.), these steps are redone to ensure engineered performance. While this was "navigational" DBMS technology and not very flexible, it was the way it was done and is the heritage of the majority of the portfolio of databases in place today. The essential point, of course, is that performance was carefully designed in for the set of predicted transactions and, conversely, no engineering was done for any other possible transactions.

If we had to do all that to assure successful operational performance with hierarchical/network databases for OLTP and OSS applications, how could we just simply superimpose SQL on top of them (assuming all the other problems were solvable) and anticipate adequate performance? An SQL optimizer optimizes the given situation; the result is relative, and does not equate to "satisfactory." It may be optimal, but that may have nothing to do with satisfactory. It would be pure coincidence that unstructured and unanticipated SQL transactions would adequately perform, and that they wouldn't disrupt the engineered performance of the navigational transactions. There is no magic.

To summarize:

1. SQL grafting would be a highly desirable technology to enable rapid client/server migration.

2. There are many data manipulation contradictions between how hierarchical and network databases permitted schema definitions and how an SQL data definition language permits schema definitions. The superimposing of SQL on a hierarchical/network database, as a consequence, has many practical barriers.

3. Even if the data structure problems could be overcome, there is good reason to believe that performance would be unsatisfactory. It would be unsatisfactory because the underlying database was carefully engineered for a specific set of transactions, while SQL will permit any proper semantic transaction. An optimizer will give the optimal access: that does not necessarily equate to adequate or satisfactory performance.

Mainframe role   (Refer to Fig. 8.11)   The central mainframe gradually migrates from the role of data manager, program development/execution environment, and presentation manager to the role of corporate resource server. Processing and presentation services are repositioned to cheaper and functionally superior processors and presenters within the client/server model. The mainframe, within the context of specialization and division of labor (see Chap. 7, Sec. 7.2), takes on roles such as data server, batch server, legacy server, and data network adminis-

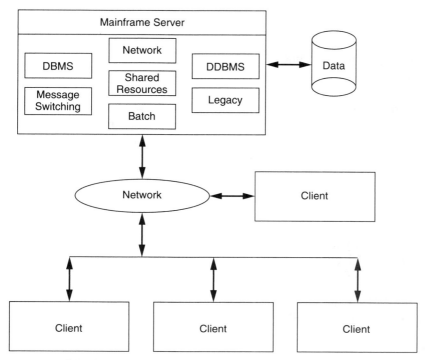

Figure 8.11   Mainframe repositioning.

tration server. One should anticipate that specialized servers based on open industry standards will compete for some of these roles. Given the large embedded base of mainframe applications (see Sec. 8.2.5 for a discussion of migration strategies), one should anticipate the repositioning to be best described as "a journey, not an event."

Advanced technology groups.   Many organizations, in order to more effectively deal with the emergence of so many new IM&M technologies, have organized Advanced Technology Groups (ATGs) with the mission of identifying and introducing new technologies in harmony with needed business capabilities. ATGs perform the following types of functions:

- technology scanning
- technology tracking
- technology analysis
- technology forecasting
- technology assessment
- technology evaluation

- technology consultation
- technology experimentation
- technology prototyping
- technology introduction

These functions are information-intensive functions and are required to be done within a "knowledge-rich" environment if technology/business-needs linking is to be accomplished in an optimal manner. ATGs require foreknowledge and position knowledge to perform this function.

It is recommended that the ATGs or equivalent function be executed within the framework of eleven information models (see Fig. 8.12) as follows:

External IM&M models. These models provide information to support tracking, analysis, assessment, and forecasting of IM&M capabilities which are/will be becoming available from the supplier community. The following four models are required:

1. *Standards model*   (Refer to Fig. 8.13.) This model is used to track the evolution of standards that influence open systems portability,

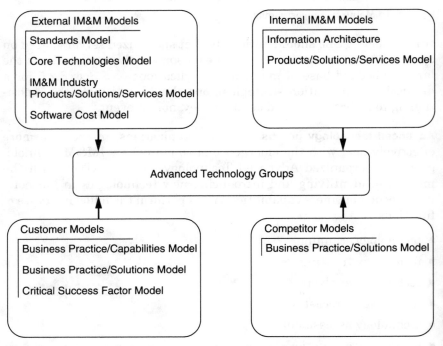

Figure 8.12   Advanced technology group information models.

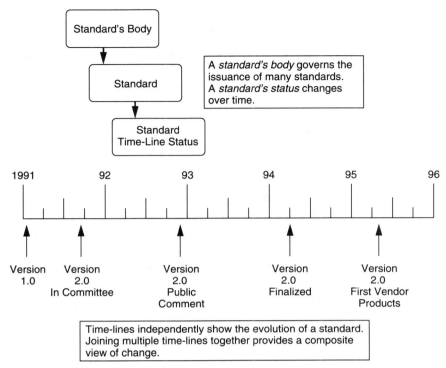

Standard's Body

Standard

A *standard's body* governs the issuance of many standards. A *standard's status* changes over time.

Standard Time-Line Status

| 1991 | 92 | 93 | 94 | 95 | 96 |

Version 1.0

Version 2.0 In Committee

Version 2.0 Public Comment

Version 2.0 Finalized

Version 2.0 First Vendor Products

Time-lines independently show the evolution of a standard. Joining multiple time-lines together provides a composite view of change.

Figure 8.13   Standards model.

scalability, interoperability, and data access. We are interested in the following types of information:

- owning standards body
- current standard and importance
- vendor implementation status of current standard
- time line of next version of standard
- opportunity/impact of next version of standard

Using this information, various time lines for a comprehensive understanding of standards and their impact can be constructed. These time lines can be merged with the other models to perform scenarios of what will be available in the future.

2. *Core technology models.*   These models identify the underlying core technologies (processor performance, storage density, communication speeds, etc.) that are the foundation of IM&M technology. For each core technology, one would like:

- raw performance time-line curve (including upper boundary of performance)

- cost/performance time-line curve
- replacement product curves for both

See Figs. 7.11, 7.12, and 7.16 for examples of these types of models. These models can be merged with each other and the other models to develop scenarios of different types of processors that will be available in the future, along with their price/performance ranges and capabilities. The upper-performance boundary limits and replacement technology information is important in anticipating when migration to new technologies will be required. This type of technology forecasting is known as S-curve analysis and is based on the S-curve cost/benefit-pattern life cycle of technologies (Fig. 8.14). Figure 8.15 illustrates how forecasts of future technology can be made by joining the discrete technology models.

3. *IM&M industry products / solutions / services model.* These models provide a thorough taxonomy (classification system) of the IM&M industry. Just as most scientific disciplines classify the subject matter to provide for structure and order, the IM&M industry needs to be similarly structured so that the change can be monitored in an orderly and comprehensive way. An example of a partial classification system would be:

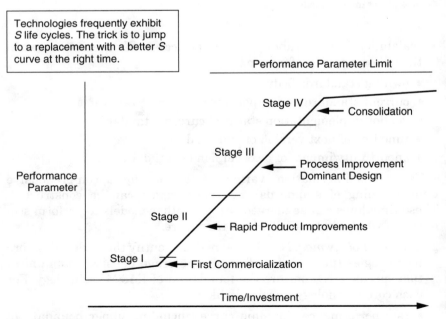

Figure 8.14 "S" curve.

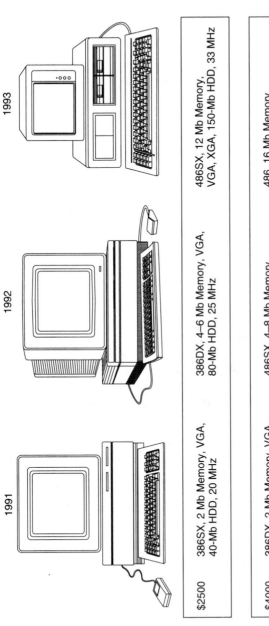

1991

$2500 — 386SX, 2 Mb Memory, VGA, 40-Mb HDD, 20 MHz

$4000 — 386DX, 2 Mb Memory, VGA, 80-Mb HDD, 33 MHz

$7000 — 486, 4 Mb Memory, VGA, 300-Mb HDD, 33 MHz

1992

386DX, 4–6 Mb Memory, VGA, 80-Mb HDD, 25 MHz

486SX, 4–8 Mb Memory, VGA/XGA, 300-Mb HDD, 33 MHz

486, 8 Mb Memory, VGA, XGA, 600-Mb HDD, 50 MHz

1993

486SX, 12 Mb Memory, VGA, XGA, 150-Mb HDD, 33 MHz

486, 16 Mb Memory, XGA, 600-Mb HDD, 50 MHz

586, 20 Mb Memory, XGA, 1-Gb HDD, 66 MHz

Figure 8.15 How much PC will you be able to buy? (*Source: IDC*)

- **Database Management Technologies**
  Database Managers

  Relational

  Object

  Network

  Hierarchical

  Inverted

- **Administration Tools**
  Sizing Aids

  Pointer Checkers

  Dump/Restore Utilities

  Restructuring Tools

  Performance Monitors

For each technology, we would like to know:

- current status
- vendor availability
- change time lines (Fig. 8.16)
- replacement technology time line

These time lines can be superimposed on each other to provide a comprehensive moving technology picture, and the other time lines to develop a composite picture of which technologies with which standards on which price/performance platforms will be available over time.

4. *Software Cost Model.*   These models provide a time-line forecast of the cost of core software components on various client/server components. By key component, client, departmental server, corporate server, etc., one would like to project the cost/MIP and/or cost/user for a chosen set of core software technologies that would include (as appropriate):

- operating system
- graphical user interface
- DBMS
- communications software
- bonding software
- security software
- telecommunications monitor

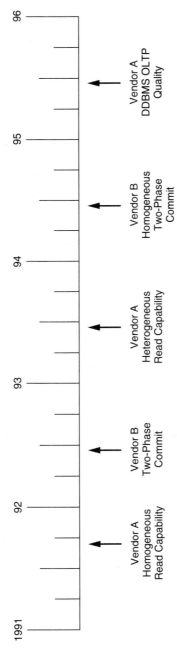

Figure 8.16 DDBMS technology timeline.

- space management tools
- administration utilities

Client/server computing is a software-based architecture as opposed to a processor-centered architecture, and understanding the changing software economics so that the impact of software costs can be managed as an asset is an important factor in understanding external IM&M trends.

Internal IM&M models. These models provide the necessary information to understand the internal IM&M solution capability. While the external models identify what exists in the marketplace and how that marketplace will evolve over time, these models center on understanding the internal capabilities of yourself as a supplier. Two models are recommended:

1. *Information architecture model.* This model defines both the logical and physical architecture that is the target infrastructure of our IM&M efforts. It defines the framework on top of which all IM&M solutions are built and enables orderly integration and migration of technologies. In addition to a data architecture and a processing architecture, a composite information architecture would also include specific standards and management practices that govern the IM&M function. The architecture should exist at both the logical and physical levels. The logical level should be long-lasting and provide constancy of purpose. The physical level should provide a set of standards that define the critical interfaces. As new technologies become available, they need to be fitted into this architecture.

2. *Product/solutions/service model.* This model provides a complete model of which IM&M capabilities are available and associated change time lines. We therefore understand what we have in stock to offer, what is being worked on, and what will be worked on. Related to each product/solution/service is the generic business practice/capability for which it is a solution. This provides linkage between IM&M and the business.

Customer models. These models provide an understanding of the requirements of IM&M by the internal users of the IM&M services. Three models are recommended:

1. *Business practice/capabilities model.* (Refer to Fig. 2.4, "Magnified Business Practice IM&M Relationship.") These models summarize the basic business capabilities to which IM&M can be applied. IM&M provides newer and newer solutions to these requirements.

2. *Business practice/solutions model.* This model links the model just mentioned in item 1 with the practice/solutions/service model.

We can therefore, in a comprehensive manner, understand which solutions are being used for which practices today and in the planned future. We fully understand our applied IM&M situation.

3. *Critical success factors model.* This model identifies which of the business practices/capabilities are viewed as priority opportunity items by the users. It therefore provides guidance in selecting new IM&M technologies for evaluation. From the external IM&M models, we would like to select emerging IM&M technologies and merge them into our information architecture and solutions for these identified business capabilities. If we can do this, we will have accomplished explicit linkage between IM&M and the business.

Competitor models. The purpose of this model is to understand how competitive suppliers to your customers provide solutions to their problems. One model is recommended as follows:

1. *Business practice / solution model.* This model, which is analogous to the customer model, would identify how competitors are solving customer problems. We can use this information to benchmark our own solutions and to continually improve them.

The preceding sets of models provide a fact-based context for evaluating and linking IM&M technology to the business. This approach offers the following advantages:

- It explicitly relates technology to the business.

- It organizes us for continuous introduction of new technology.

- It permits us to anticipate change and to make sure that all the changes will "fit" together.

- It eliminates the "fog of technology" that is often associated with the IM&M function.

While one could persuasively argue that this type of approach was always needed to plan IM&M, the problems it addresses become more exaggerated with client/server computing. Open systems will result in waves of new products that will have to be integrated. The IM&M organization will have to deal with, for example, inter-LAN router/ bridge/brouter connections, parallel processing, DDBMS, full multimedia, work-flow management software, CASE/repositories, imaging, and voice processing. It will therefore be more important than ever to understand:

- exactly what we have to offer
- what works with what

- what the ripple effect of change will be
- which change is coming when
- which changes benefit the business
- how we can constantly improve our solutions

This cannot be done as an event. It has to be done as a continuous structured process.

Figure 8.17 illustrates an operational flow for an ATG. Since ATGs need to rapidly bring in new technology for specific advantageous applications, the flow permits both an expedient implementation effort for the limited exploitation of the technology and a complete plan for the thorough integration of the technology into the IM&M portfolio.

The fluid introduction of advantageous technologies will become even more important with the client/server environment. ATGs need to perform their function based on facts, not on opinion or good fortune.

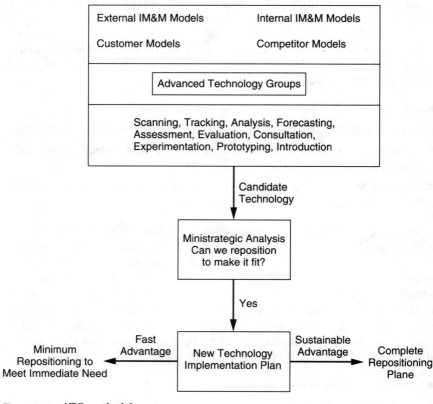

Figure 8.17   ATG methodology.

... so what enables an intelligent leadership to achieve extraordinary accomplishments is foreknowledge. Foreknowledge cannot be gotten from ghosts and spirits, cannot be had by analogy, nor can it be found out by calculation. It must be obtained from people, people who know the conditions of the enemy.*

8.2.3   Organization structure

The purpose of this section is to analyze how the IM&M organization should reorganize to best support the paradigm shift to client/server computing. Figure 8.18 illustrates a typical IM&M organization structure and the associated functions performed. The obvious question is: "Why that structure?" We would assert that that structure was predominant because it properly serviced the host architecture computing model that it was designed to support. It was designed with the following in mind:

- Host-based processing is uniprocessor-oriented.

- Each processing technology was a self-contained and supported smokestack with self-contained applications.

- Each environment was defined by the processing technology.

- Each environment was closed (proprietary products).

- There was little concern for:

    portability
    interoperability
    cooperative processing
    build here but run there
    cross environment configuration management

The traditional structure was therefore quite reasonable. But will it adequately service client/server computing?

Table 8.2 can help answer that question. It would appear that the attributes of the new environment are radically different. The organization structure will require restructuring to effectively support the client/server environment that has such different attributes. The unsuitability of the traditional structure to support client/server computing has been manifesting itself for years. As illustrated in Fig. 8.19, when the IM&M processing architectures (see Chap. 4, Sec. 4.3) are measured against the traditional organization structure, suitability declines as the requirements for distribution/cooperation increase. The IM&M organization has, in effect, been feeling the strains of its legacy structure for years. But the question is: how to restructure?

---

* *The Art of War* by Sun Tzu.

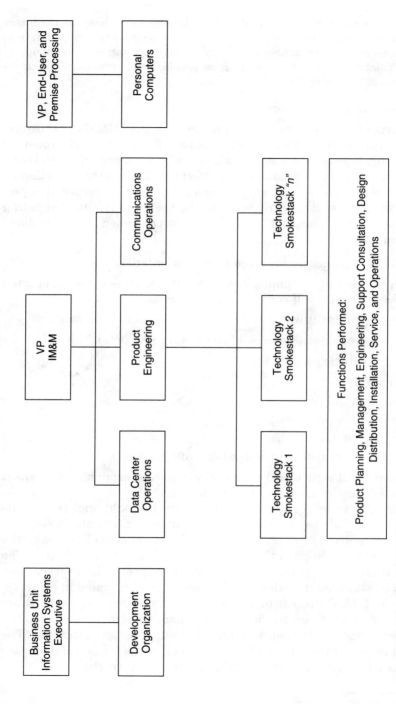

Figure 8.18 Traditional IM&M organization structure.

TABLE 8.2   Comparison: Host-Centered Computing versus Client/Server Computing

Since Client/Server Attributes Are So Different, the Organization Structure Will Have to Be Repositioned (Restructured) to Reflect Client/Server Requirements

Host-centered computing	Client/server computing
Uniprocessor orientation	Multiple processor orientation
Self-contained environments	Interoperability
Hardware-centered architecture	Software-centered architecture
Proprietary products	Open systems and standards
Homogeneous environment	Heterogeneous environment
"A" primary vendor	Mix/match suppliers
Little portability	Portability key advantage
Dumb client	Intelligent clients
Development and production environments equate	Build here—run there
Vertical configuration management (often provided by vendor)	Horizontal configuration management (provided by you)
Product engineering (systems support) function in "parts" business	Product engineering function in systems integration business

Organization design insights from IM&M technology.   Superior technologies are founded on superior ideas. Can we learn about a better organization structure for IM&M by gaining insight from relational DBMS technology, client/server computing, configuration management, and object-oriented design? From each of these, we will identify an underlying superior idea and a maxim for restructuring.

Relational DBMS.   (See Fig. 8.20.)
Idea: Normalized table structures can be dynamically joined by common keys. This allows for creating both anticipated and unanticipated new tables.

Maxim: Horizontal client/server solutions will require joining multiple IM&M disciplines and skills together in anticipated and unanticipated ways. Think of organizational units as relational entities that are joined as required to create newer and newer client/server solutions.

Client/server computing.   (See Fig. 7.3.)
Idea: Decouple presentation, processing, and data layers of applications to permit accessibility, shareability, reusability, and functional specialization.

Maxim: Organize by function (not by technology) to permit reusability, depth of function, and end-to-end product management, design, engineering, and operations.

Configuration management.   (See Fig. 8.21.)
Idea: Configuration management is the discipline of identifying and controlling the configuration of a system in order to systemati-

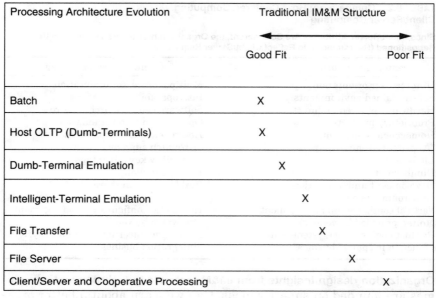

Processing Architecture Evolution	Traditional IM&M Structure	
	Good Fit	Poor Fit
Batch	X	
Host OLTP (Dumb-Terminals)	X	
Dumb-Terminal Emulation	X	
Intelligent-Terminal Emulation	X	
File Transfer	X	
File Server		X
Client/Server and Cooperative Processing		X

Figure 8.19 Processing architecture versus organization structure.

cally control its definition as it undergoes continual modification. Any set of components which work together to deliver a composite service is a *configuration*. Configuration management is the discipline/process of moving a component's inventory from a certified configuration at time T_1 to another certified configuration at time T_2. This is analogous to the database technology idea of "committing" a transaction; all the changes commit in harmony, or none commit. The entire configuration inventory has to move from one consistent state to another consistent state.

Maxim: Client/server solutions should be viewed as sets of products (configurations) that have to be managed as individual parts,

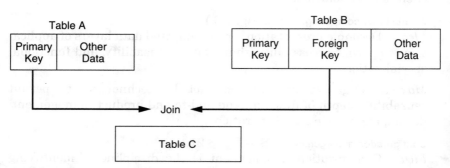

Figure 8.20 Relational DBMS.

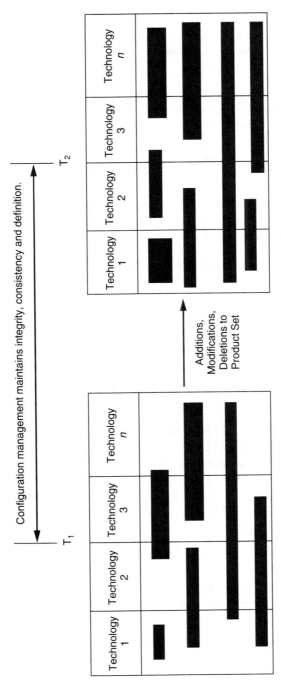

Figure 8.21 Configuration management.

assemblies, and superassemblies. The planning function must maintain the integrity and consistency of the complete part, assembly, or superassembly set of solutions as client/server solutions evolve over time.

Object-oriented design.   (See Fig. 8.22.)

Idea: An object is the center of attention and is encapsulated by methods that define the permitted functions against the object.

Maxim: IM&M service functions, planning, engineering, support, etc., should be viewed as methods that encapsulate the object "product."

Restructuring suggestions.   Based on these technological insights and the other information provided about client/server computing and its attributes, we recommend the following actions:

1. Organize by function as opposed to by technology (Fig. 8.23). The essence of client/server computing is end-to-end horizontal interoperability. The IM&M organization should be coordinated to plan, engineer, distribute, operate, etc. the entire project.

2. Position units as clients and servers to each other (Fig. 8.24). This will provide for clean interfaces between horizontal functions and permit joining of functions as required in task teams.

3. The planning function should oversee the administration of a product inventory system to ensure definition and consistency of products (Fig. 8.25). Traditional manufacturing functions such as bill-of-materials, parts implosions, parts explosion, and master scheduling must be implemented to permit orderly control of horizontal integration. Figure 8.26 attempts to illustrate the vital importance of configuration management in the client/server world. To achieve any

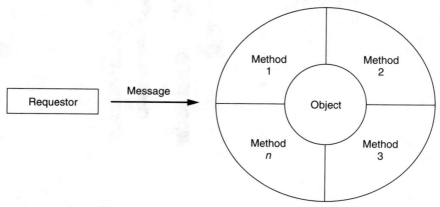

Figure 8.22   Object-oriented design.

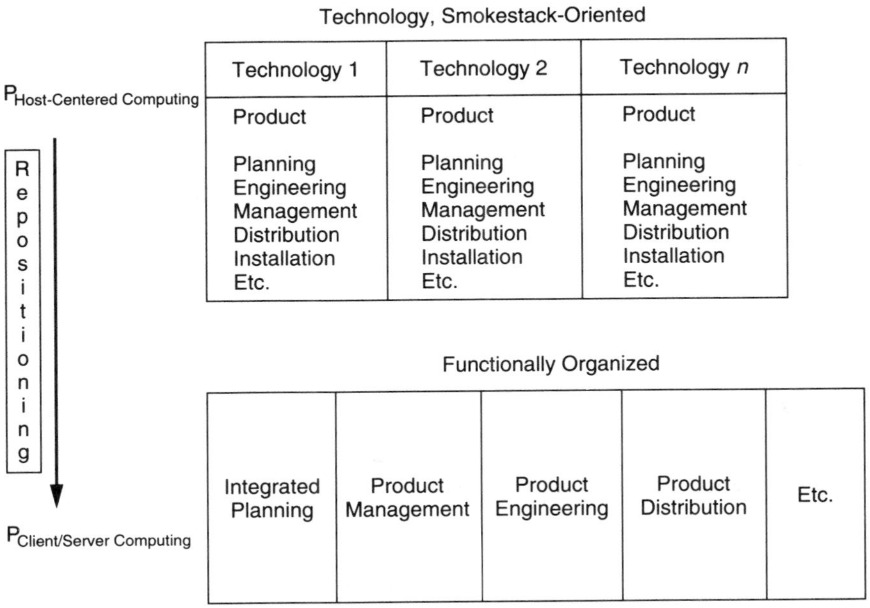

Technology, Smokestack-Oriented

	Technology 1	Technology 2	Technology *n*
	Product	Product	Product
	Planning	Planning	Planning
	Engineering	Engineering	Engineering
	Management	Management	Management
	Distribution	Distribution	Distribution
	Installation	Installation	Installation
	Etc.	Etc.	Etc.

P$_{Host-Centered Computing}$

R
e
p
o
s
i
t
i
o
n
i
n
g

Functionally Organized

Integrated Planning	Product Management	Product Engineering	Product Distribution	Etc.

P$_{Client/Server Computing}$

Figure 8.23   Functional organization structure.

economies of scale, solutions will have to be layered on top of solutions. This will create a complicated dependency tree that will require careful impact analysis and control to ensure the integrity of all offerings as the individual parts go through evolution. Without a parts inventory to support configuration management, how will you ever know what works with what?

4. View the product in the product inventory as the central object of IM&M, and all the business functions as methods that operate on it (Fig. 8.27). Functions interface with each other by well-defined interfaces, and they operate on a common product inventory.

8.2.4   Human resources

The purpose of this section is to analyze the impact that client/server computing has on the information-technology professional. Of vital importance to repositioning the IM&M professional are the issues of competencies (skills), values/behaviors, and training (education). Each will be discussed separately.

Competencies (skills).   The Core Competency Model* (Fig. 8.28) provides a framework to relate competencies to products. The model

---

* *The Core Competencies of the Corporation,* G. Hamel and C. Prahalad, HBR, May/June 1990.

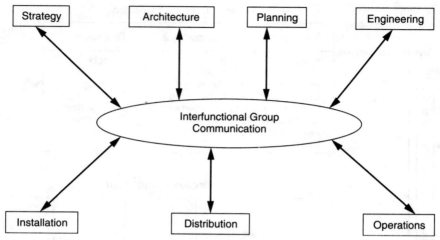

Figure 8.24　Functional units as clients and servers.

suggests that core competencies are the roots of core products from which many business and end products grow. Figure 8.29 shows the migration in skills required of the IM&M professionals in light of client/server computing. Historically, skills were required in the following disciplines:

- processing
- data communications
- data management
- application development
- knowledge engineering

To support client/server computing, the following three competencies must be added:

1. *Process management.* Process management is the planning, design, execution, and control of processes. As discussed in the previous section, it will be necessary to deliver end-to-end horizontal technology solutions. This will require the development of sophisticated processes to coordinate the life-cycle management of solutions.

2. *Applied information movement and management.* In migrating from the technologist's perspective to the business perspective, the IM&M professional will need to evolve to become a business consultant. The trick is the advantageous exploitation of IM&M technology. Who knows better than the IM&M professional how to work with users to apply the technology? This is a means to achieving linkage between the business and IM&M.

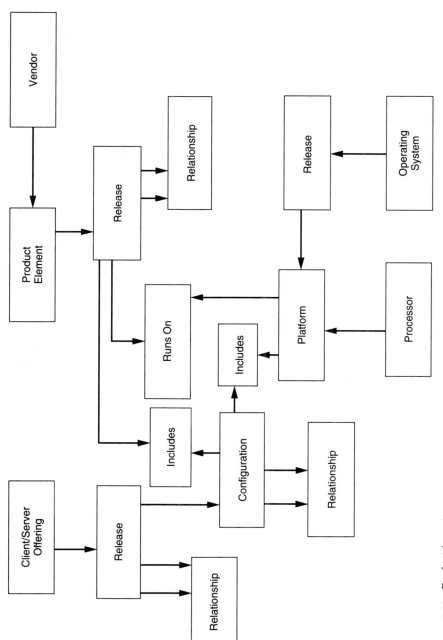

Figure 8.25 Product inventory.

213

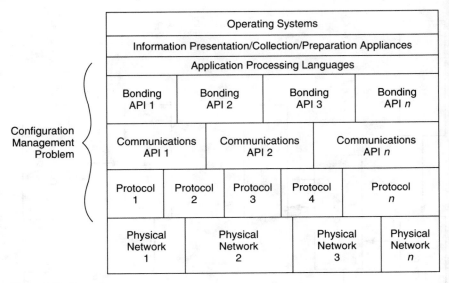

Figure 8.26 Layering.

3. *Systems integration.*   Historically, IM&M units were in the parts business and, often, the problem of integration belonged primarily to the proprietary supplier. With client/server computing, IM&M becomes a full-fledged systems integrator. The nature of systems integration, as delineated by Hopkins, is as follows:

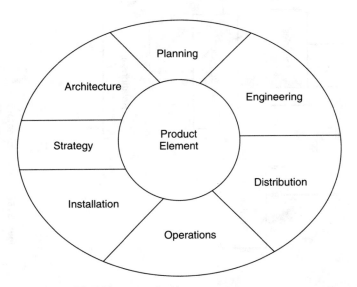

Figure 8.27 The object organization.

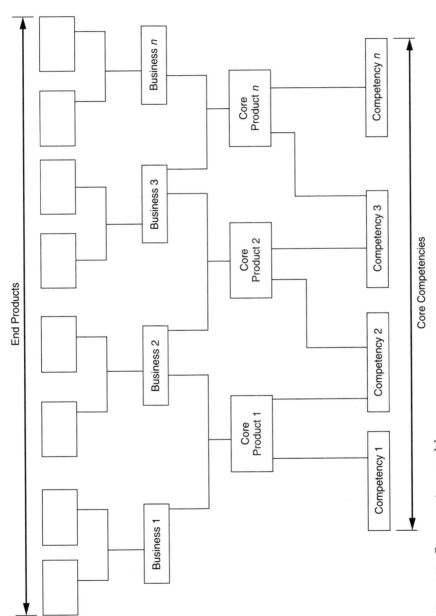

Figure 8.28 Core competency model.

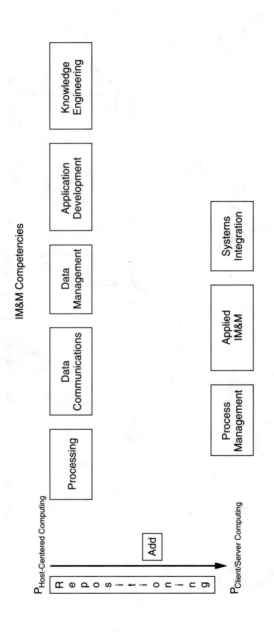

Figure 8.29 IM&M competency repositioning.

(a) The whole is primary and the parts are secondary.

(b) Integration is the condition of the interrelationships of the many parts within it.

(c) The parts so constitute an indissoluble whole that no part can be affected without affecting all other parts.

(d) The nature of the part and its function is derived from its position in the whole, and its behavior is regulated by the whole to part relationship.

(e) Parts play their role in the light of the purpose for which the whole exists.

(f) Everything should start with the whole as a premise, and the parts and relationships should evolve.*

The mastery of configuration management (Fig. 8.21) cannot be overemphasized and will be further discussed in Sec. 8.2.7, where the development of a configuration-management system will be discussed as a required infrastructure investment along with a high-speed peer-to-peer network.

Values/behaviors.   To be successful in the competitive environment of the 1990s and to deal with the constant influx of new technologies, more than ever IM&M professionals will need to exercise the behaviors of winners. Figure 8.30 applies the core competency model to the issue of human resource management. Competencies are replaced by winning values; the human resource systems equate to the core products and serve the strategic purpose of reinforcing winning behaviors; and the end products equate to the winning behaviors.

As part of repositioning, we would like to revise the human resource systems to have a dual purpose: (1) their classical tactical purpose that is the administration of a human resource function and (2) a strategic purpose which is the influencing and reinforcement of winning behaviors. An implementation program would proceed as follows:

- Identify corporate value set.

- Identify desired winning behaviors.

- Inventory current human resource systems and identify tactical purpose of each.

- Matrix the winning behaviors to the inventoried human resource systems to decide which systems must be reengineered to explicitly reinforce the winning behaviors.

- Perform a barrier analysis (see Sec. 8.2.8) to minimize obstacles.

---

* *Integration: Its Meaning and Application,* L. Thomas Hopkins, Appleton-Century Crofts, 1937.

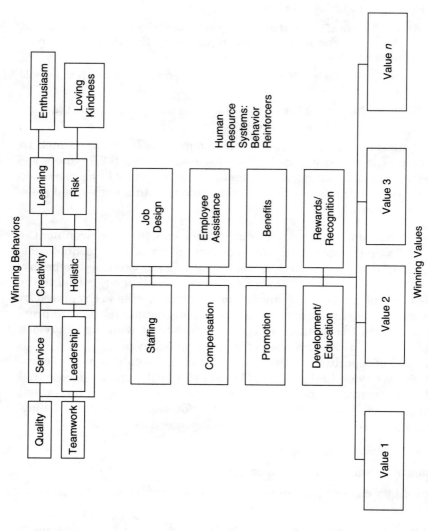

Figure 8.30 Human resources systems: values and culture architecture.

- Prioritize reengineering based on payoffs and logical sequence.
- Implement.

The human resource systems now have two purposes:

1. a tactical purpose that is to administer the targeted human resource area
2. a strategic purpose that is to reinforce winning behaviors

Education.   The nature of a paradigm shift is *big* change. It should be obvious that the discontinuities will be unsettling to the staff. The staff requires general education on what is going on (the "mega" paradigm-shift view), the overall repositioning plan (what we're doing), and reskilling as required. Much of what current IM&M professionals know, especially their host-centered view of the world, is becoming more obsolete each day. Reeducation coupled with the repositioning of the human resource systems are important actions to energize the staff for the necessary changes that will be surrounding them.

8.2.5   Information systems

The purpose of this section is to provide suggestions on how the IM&M organization can gradually migrate to the client/server environment. If we had the luxury of a "desert start," it would be simple: just build everything new within the model. Unfortunately, we have a "jungle start" and have to carry forward our heritage. So the problem is "How do we migrate from the kludge of architectures and closed databases to the client/server world?"

We would suggest the following seven basic actions:

1. *Information architecture.*   The host-centered architectural mess was nothing compared to the potential client/server mess if a proper architecture is not put in place. It is imperative to see that the infrastructure that will bond you is defined.

   The information architecture is the "client/server product." One does not buy a client/server product as one has traditionally purchased a DBMS, editor, or screen painter. The client/server product consists of client processors, the bonding products, the networks, the servers, and, most importantly, the APIs that are the plugs to which programs on both sides attach in order to create the illusion of oneness. How could one implement client/server computing without a defined architecture?

2. *Data administration.*   The inelegance of batch "data scrubbers" is nothing compared to the problems of client/server users accessing

incompatible data definitions from multiple data servers. It is imperative that data be treated as a critical corporate resource and that its definition be put under data administration control. A datum is the most basic point of interface, and the reunification of the corporate schema will never take place unless agreement is reached on the definition of each data element.

3. *Layered development.* Develop all new software within the framework of a presentation, processing, and data layer with strict interfaces. This will facilitate the later partitioning of the application into clients and servers.

4. *Bridging.* Treat the embedded base of databases and file systems as legacy servers. Exploit the adaptability of client/server computing (Fig. 7.3) to move presentation and processing away from the host.

5. *Decision-support architecture.* Put the decision-support database architecture in place. Using extracts from the collage of OLTP and OSS databases, implement the client/server environment with the About-the-Business Applications.

    Using this approach, implementation is usually less disruptive than it would be in the production environment, is more easily accomplished, and delivers decision-improvement payoffs. Many activities that will differentiate companies in the 1990s (such as strategy development, quality improvement, productivity design, competitive analysis, and product design) are all information-intensive practices.

6. *Revalue your legacy.* The current value of the embedded base of applications is equal to its replacement value, not its original development cost. In light of the following, the cost of redoing (certainly of redoing the critical business practices) may not be as overwhelming as first anticipated:

   - improved feature/functionality through reengineering of the business
   - changing computing economics
   - reusability through servers
   - improved development productivity through modern CASE development methods

7. *Stepping-stone OSS/OLTP servers.* Under proper data administration, build OLTP and OSS subject databases as decoupled servers that are accessed through the client/server architecture. As DDBMS technology matures, create logical servers by superimposing DDBMS on the servers that are compatible (due to proper data administration) and accessible (due to the client/server architecture).

Unfortunately, as was discussed in Sec. 8.2.2 regarding SQL grafting, there is no magic. The embedded base is a drag on what could be achieved, but it *is* the embedded base and won't disappear. These approaches, plus improvements in reengineering software, will provide reasonable mechanisms to an orderly migration.

8.2.6 Management systems

Management systems are the frameworks within which the management team runs the business. We recommend the following to support the paradigm shift:

- *Strategic planning.* The strategic planning framework should be implemented, if it hasn't been already. As change gains momentum, it will be more important than ever to attempt to anticipate the impacts of IM&M technology on the enterprise. The strategic planning model provides a framework to accomplish that. It should also be noted that the notion of "repositioning" is a very powerful basis for factual discussions. It moves the debate from opinion, hearsay, and wishful thinking to what is and what will probably be, and crosses the gap between the two.

- *Quality.* As was stated in Sec. 3.2, Deming standards and the Baldrige Award are the "ante" to play the game. The requirement of systems integration, however, forces the issue. Without quality suppliers, quality processes, quality-oriented staff, and quality support systems (such as configuration management), holding the distributed world together will be nearly impossible.

- *Competitor analysis.* The internal IM&M organization has more competitors now than at any time in its history. Not only is there the viable out-sourcing threat (EDS, CSC, IBM, AAC) but, more and more, the user organizations will suspect that they can do it themselves (the ultimate in-sourcing). Resources should be devoted to understanding what your competitors are doing. This benchmarking provides a means to assess the value of your services and to strive for continual improvement.

- *Applying IM&M to the IM&M business functions.* In many companies, the IM&M organization is the least automated. Just like any other business function, the IM&M organization has business practices, capability requirements, and critical business practices. IM&M should be exploited to improve the functioning of the IM&M organization on a continual basis just as it is used to improve the other parts of the business.

  Figure 8.31 illustrates the emerging way that organizations manage their products and services. It is called a *dual sun system* since all the other functions and services revolve around the "two suns" of product management and account management. This obviously provides a strong hint of what should be automated first: information about the products (the configuration management system) and information about the customers (business practices, capabilities, in-use solutions, and critical success factors). These activities feed the ATGs (Sec. 8.2.2) much of the vital "model" information they need to link new technology to the business.

8.2.7 Sustainable competitive advantage

Certain strategic initiatives transcend cost justification. This is because they have strategic value which is not easily translated into a monetary presentation. In moving to client/server computing, there are three infrastructure investments which have this strategic value attribute. They are (1) a high bandwidth peer-to-peer network, (2) a configuration management system, and (3) an end-to-end operations, administration, and maintenance capability. Each will be discussed separately.

High bandwidth peer-to-peer network. Client/server computing will cause an explosion in peer-to-peer network traffic—an explosion that can be anticipated. Most enterprises have synchronous, asynchronous, or file transfer networks in place. These will not be adequate for the flood of traffic that we want to occur. A peer-to-peer network to support/ enable the client/server environment is a strategic investment much like the construction of a national highway, railroads, or airports. While much of the remaining investment can be done in a graduated manner, this requires a deep up-front commitment. As Thomas Kuhn suggests, adopting a paradigm shift is done partly on faith. Part of that faith is

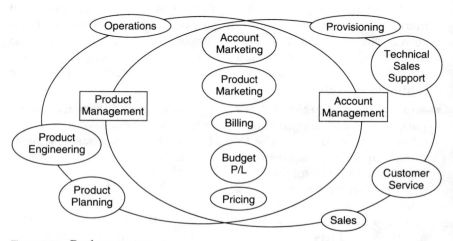

Figure 8.31 Dual sun system.

the construction of the necessary infrastructure communications capability to enable the peer-to-peer traffic.

Configuration management system. By the time that a configuration management system can be completely cost-justified through the obvious pain of the IM&M staff, it will be too late. It is simply a capability requirement of the paradigm shift. If you are going into the systems-integration business, you require a core system to manage the whole and the parts. The importance of a configuration management system can not be overstressed.

End-to-end operations, administration, and maintenance capability. As was illustrated in Fig. 7.7, "IM&M Architecture of the 1990s," the processing architecture of client/server computing is networks of networks. Those organizations that can provision, operate, administer, and maintain that environment in all its dimensions will have a distinct advantage.

These investments are of prime importance because they provide the basis for the IM&M organization's contribution to building sustainable competitive advantage. They break the bottlenecks by delivering the client/server environment. By putting in place these capabilities, the IM&M organization will be positioned to meet the true business requirement of IM&M: the ability to maneuver.

8.2.8 Repositioning summary

This section has analyzed the major issues involved in repositioning the organization in response to the paradigm shift. Viewed from this perspective, it is clear that the implementation of client/server computing is much more than a technology transfer problem: it requires a strategic implementation to reposition all impacted strategic areas in harmony with the new paradigm.

Table 8.3 summarizes the major issues requiring management attention, along with recommended actions. For each implementation issue, it is necessary to develop appropriate implementation programs to bridge the gap from your current position to the client/server position. The barrier analysis results and the comment strategy should be exploited to make crossing the gap easier.

The overall approach to repositioning can be understood as follows:

- For each implementation issue within strategic area, determine the current organizational position. To the degree possible, present that position either graphically, quantitatively, or (if qualitatively) explicitly.

- For each implementation issue within strategic area, determine the desired organizational position. Present the target position using the same presentation media as that used for the current position.

TABLE 8.3   Repositioning Summary

Implementation Programs Are Required to Operationalize Recommended Actions

Strategic area	Implementation issue	Recommend action
Supplier	Out-sourcing	Utility functions only
	Vendor Relationship Management	Deming partner
	Single supplier for everything	Tactical implementation strategy
Technology	SQL grafting mainframe role	Low probability of corporate server success
	Advanced technology groups	Link technology to business capability requirements through use of models
Organization structure	Organization redesign	Functional organization structure
Human resources	Education core competencies	Massive reeducation Add process management program, applied IM&M consulting, and systems integration
	Values/behaviors	Reengineer human resource systems to reinforce positive behaviors driven from values
Information systems	Migration to client/server architecture	1. Develop an information architecture 2. Implement data administration 3. Do layered development 4. Bridge to legacy databases using adaptive client/server partitioning alternatives 5. Do decision support first 6. Revalue your embedded base of systems 7. Build OSS and OLTP servers and then link them by DDBMS
Management systems	Strategic planning	Do strategic planning
	Quality commitment	Insist on quality
	Competitor analysis	Benchmark to constantly improve
	Apply IM&M to self	Use IM&M to infuse competitive advantage into own processes
Sustainable competitive advantage	Peer-to-peer network	Strategic investment
	Configuration management system	Strategic investment
	End-to-end operations, administration and maintenance capability	Strategic investment

- Define a set of implementation projects to close the gap.
- Use the barrier analysis and commitment strategy to ease the pain of change.
- Divide the effort into multiple strategic-planning cycles.

There is much to be done.

8.3 Conclusions

The migration of the information-systems architecture to client/server computing from host-centered computing is not simply a technology transfer problem—it is a paradigm shift. Paradigm shifts demand major repositioning. Simply introducing client/server technologies without making the necessary changes in the other affected strategic areas will not be sufficient. A new position in harmony with client/server needs to be realized.

One must thoughtfully and thoroughly analyze the current situation of the IM&M asset and develop an insightful and comprehensive plan for a complete implementation—a plan which includes the necessary realignment of all the impacted strategic areas. The deeper your plan, the greater your success. In the words of Sun Tzu:

> When your strategy is deep and far reaching, then what you gain by your calculations is much, so you can win before you even fight. When your strategic thinking is shallow and nearsighted, then what you gain by your calculations is little, so you lose before you do battle. Much strategy prevails over little strategy, so those with no strategy cannot but be defeated. Therefore it is said that victorious warriors win first and then go to war, while defeated warriors go to war first and then seek to win.*

Master Sun is, of course, right. How else could it be? You need an implementation plan which has succeeded before you execute it. Remember what Machiavelli warned at the beginning of this chapter. There will be many who have prospered under the old paradigm and will resist with great force the repositioning. By "gaining much" during your planning, you can win, not by good fortune or brute force, but by intelligence.

> . . . So it is said that good warriors take their stand on ground where they cannot lose . . . ground where one cannot lose is invincible strategy that makes it impossible for your opponent to defeat you*

Gain much during your calculations: think holistically, anticipate barriers, and commit yourself to the undertaking.

---

* *The Art of War,* Sun Tzu.

9

Epilogue

During the period following the publication of my book on application prototyping, I was invited to speak at a conference on "Structured Methods." As the subjects normally covered at this type of conference were data flow diagrams, structure charts, functional decomposition and such, they were inviting the heretic to speak to the most pious. After I gave my presentation as the keynote speaker, a particularly zealous adherent to the "theology" of Bubble Diagrams denounced my ideas vociferously. He was joined with enthusiasm by many of his colleagues. My response was to ask a few simple questions: "Does what you're advocating work? Having deforested half of Montana and Idaho at the altar of motionless specifications, *does it work?* Do you build systems that, when implemented, meet the business-practice needs? Or do you enter a painful period of expensive and demoralizing rework? Though you didn't intend to, did you not build a prototype anyway—only a terribly expensive one?" What is so heretical about a working model?

A similar candid self-examination would appear advantageous to the subject now at hand. Is the linkage between IM&M and the business as ill as has been suggested? Are the pathologies depleting our ability to compete? Do the pathologies place such a drag on your efforts that adaptation and maneuverability are impossible? Can you act and react promptly and purposefully? There is no sanctuary or safe harbor, so be honest.

Client/server computing provides a treatment plan for many of the problems that have been examined in this book. Since its impact is major and its effect will be lasting, its domain is strategic. It provides a path to competitive superiority through positioning for current advantage and adaptability for future advantage. Competitive success is not simply good fortune; it is not just the role of the dice. If you do not take action to revise the IM&M architecture of your system's portfolio to the client/server model and your competitors do (and they will), you will surely have lost before the game has even begun. Winners win by pre-positioning themselves advantageously. Repetitive success is not an accident.

> . . . Their victories are not flukes. Their victories are not flukes because they position themselves where they will surely win: prevailing over those who have already lost.*

Client/server computing has already won, and host-centered computing has already lost. The ascent of the client/server architecture as the predominant processing architecture of the 1990s is a fait accompli. The implementation, though just begun, is an anticlimax. Client/server computing is a fait accompli because it better solves the enduring and foundation business requirement of competitive advantage with superior price/performance and new feature/functionality. It provides the business with the maximum reach and range to operationalize business decisions. Figure 9.1 restates Fig. 3.5 ("Reach and Range"), but identifies it for what it really is: the playing field on which IM&M competitive advantage is won or lost based on the maneuverability of the architecture-dependent business applications. Which playing piece do you choose? The days of decision are now; embrace the paradigm shift and prosper, or drive fast forward with your eyes glued to the rearview mirror and witness, within a few years, a moribund organization. Always remember, complacency is the worst position of all: "It is easy to take over from those who do not plan ahead."*

---

* *The Art of War,* Sun Tzu.

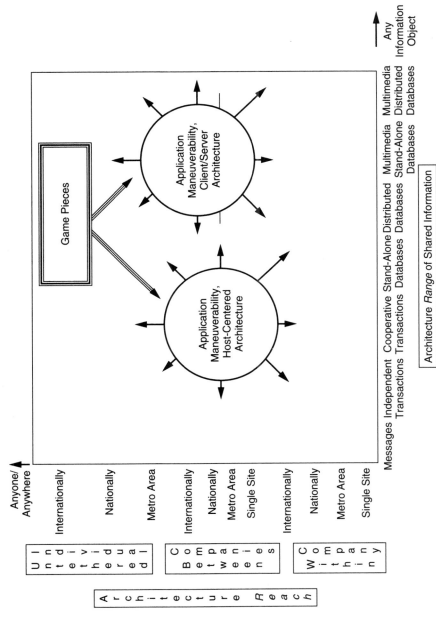

Figure 9.1 The IM&M competitive advantage game board.

Index

ABOUT THE AUTHOR

Bernard H. Boar has more than 20 years of information technology experience both within AT&T and as a consultant. His areas of expertise include software development, prototyping, strategic information systems planning, and DBMS technology. He has written a number of important professional papers in these areas, and is also the author of *Abend Debugging for Cobol Programmers* and *Application Prototyping: A Requirements Definition Strategy for the '80s*. He currently works as a strategic information technology planner at AT&T (Piscataway, New Jersey) and resides with his family in East Brunswick, New Jersey.